Between
U and Me

Between U and Me

How to Rock Your Tween Years with Style and Confidence

BY ZENDAYA

WITH SHERYL BERK

Disney • HYPERION BOOKS

NEW YORK

To my nieces and nephews (or as I like to call them, my little munchkins) who are, most likely, gonna need this book in a few years, so I hope Auntie can help!

❋

Contents

Introduction

Hey, Zendaya here! Maybe you've seen me as Rocky on the Disney Channel show *Shake It Up*. Or maybe you've heard my song "Swag It Out." Besides all the stuff you may think you know about me, I'm here to tell you I am just a normal girl—and I've been through a lot of the same stuff you're dealing with right now. Like school . . . and friends . . . and figuring out what to wear every day. Being a tween is tough—I know this because, just a few years ago, I felt like my life was one big hot mess. I remember back in fifth grade, life was very "drama-full." I didn't feel like I was really myself yet—I was shy and quiet, which is weird, because I am so not like that now! But back then, I was just following the pack, trying to fit in and figure out who I was. I was caught in all these circles and cliques, and I looked like a copy of everyone else (if they wore Abercrombie and Juicy, so did I), even though I knew it wasn't the real me.

Here's the thing about the Tween Years: You're not a little kid anymore, but you're not quite a teenager, either. What you are is just stuck somewhere between the ages of eight and twelve, and stuck doesn't feel great. It's kind of like being in a foreign place without a GPS! But here's the thing: sometimes when you have no idea where you are going, you discover a really cool new place you would never have found otherwise!

When I hit the double digits, everything seemed to change, and things got complicated. Gone were the days of playdates and Barbies. Suddenly, there were mean girls in the yard, cute boys in class, and lots of angst and "uh-oh, what is goin' on with my body?" I felt like no one really "got" me a hundred percent—or at least the new me I was growing into. So that left me to pretty much figure things out for myself. I remember thinking at the time, "Gee, wouldn't it be cool if there were some magic fairy godmother who just popped in whenever I needed her advice?" But this is reality, and you have to go through the tween years to come out on the other side wiser and on your way to being a mature adult.

I don't have a magic wand handy, but what I do have is my experiences to share with you in this book. I promise I will be totally honest and tell it to you like it is. Stuff like zits, girl drama, crushes, first-day-of-school nerves, and proving to your parents you are mature enough to cross the street without holding their hands. I'll also try my very best to answer your toughest questions—you know, the ones you're too embarrassed to ask your friends, family, or teachers? Fire away! Thanks to my Web site, I've gotten thousands of letters from all of you asking so many different things. I had lots of great questions to choose from.

I can't guarantee that my book—or any book, for that matter—will make all your problems go away. But I will promise you this: you're not alone out there. There are moments when every kid feels scared, lost, confused, overwhelmed, ugly, and weird. Even me. Okay, especially me! There were times I felt like my emotions were just running crazy—anything could make me cry, anything could make me laugh. Sound familiar? With all these things going on at once, it can be a lot to handle!

Here's the good news: this "young life crisis" you feel like you're going through? It's gonna pass. I can say that now; I'm a wise woman of sixteen! But seriously, I had to go through a lot to get where I am. And that's okay, because making mistakes is how you grow. Just DFTS—don't forget to smile. Beyond that, just believe in yourself, in your ideas, in your dreams. You don't have to dance to anyone else's beat except your own. If you don't like what everyone else is doing, then go ahead and shake things up a little! You don't have to be anything but the best YOU you can be. Trust me—I've been in your sneakers before. I understand not just what you're going through, but how it feels. And if you're like me, you hate lame advice from "experts." You want a big sister/best friend to lay it out for you and put things in perspective. I volunteer! And I promise, I'll keep your secrets (if you'll keep mine!).

This is just between you and me. . . .

Chapter 1

BFFs

I could not deal without my friends.

Seriously, I don't know what I would do without them. These are the people who put up with my craziness (and kinda like it!); they understand my hectic schedule and don't complain (that often). They listen to my dreams and encourage me to chase them. My friends are the glue that holds me together. I know that anytime I need my friends, they're a phone call away—and they'll do anything for me because I would do anything for them. I had a really challenging dance to do for an episode recently, and my two best friends were here and not only helped me practice, but they also cheered me on from behind the scenes. I couldn't have done it without them!

When I was in elementary school, I made new friends every year with kids in my class. I don't know about you, but I wasn't all that picky back then. Anyone who gave me a sticker or shared her snack was my new bestie. Middle school is different; it's when the right friends matter the most. Tween friendship is more intimate and involved because things are way more complicated. Your life is filled with challenges and emotions. You want to be noticed, but you also want to fit in. Cliques get cliquier; stresses get more stressful. And that's all before you even tackle your classes (exams, term papers, and homework . . . oh, my!). At the same time, you're trying to show your parents that you're a big kid now and you can handle it—even when you can't.

The good news is good friends—make that *great* friends—will see you through everything. They are your sounding board, your cheerleading squad, your cross-my-heart-hope-to-die secret keepers. You may rely on an old one you've known since preschool or lean on a new one you met in homeroom. The point is, this person is going to have your back no matter how long you've known him or her.

A good friend is someone who . . .

 won't judge you because you're having a bad hair day

 knows that what makes you different makes you beautiful

 helps you up when you fall flat on your face in heels

 shares their one and only last scoop of ice cream with you

 stays up all night with you sharing secrets and telling stories

 thinks it's okay to be lazy or crazy sometimes

 defends you when someone puts you down

is hard to come by

Keep your besties close and cherish them!

Making Friends 101

How cool would it be if they actually taught this class in school? It's not as tough as you might think. Above all, be the kind of friend you would like to make.

- **Act friend-ly.** Sounds like a given, right? Be warm, open, encouraging. When I'm in a room with strangers, I like to be the icebreaker, the one who goes up to everyone and says, "Hey, I'm Zendaya. What's up? How ya doin'?" I used to be a lot more shy, but I learned that standing in a corner and not making any eye contact was not going to win me any friends. If you're not comfortable chatting up people, then at least look them in the eye, smile, and say hi. It's just two little letters, one tiny little word—and it goes a very long way.

- **Find someone similar.** I don't mean a lookalike or some girl in your algebra class rocking the same pair of jeans. I mean make friends with people you have something in common with. Sign up for activities or after-school clubs so you can meet people who share your interests and hobbies. I did a lot of hanging with the kids who liked performing and acting—and obviously all the actors on *Shake*

It Up are my closest pals because we have that in
common and spend so much time together.

- **Make a date.** Sometimes you need a little one-
on-one time to form a connection. Offer to do
homework together, grab a slice, or catch a movie
on a weekend. Don't make it a huge deal. Just ask,
"Hey, are you free after school?"

- **Have another friend introduce you.** There's
nothing wrong with asking an old pal if you can
hang with her and her new circle of friends. There
may be a time when you can do the same for her. I
always say, "The more the merrier." Just be warned:
some kids can be a bit possessive of their pals. If
she doesn't want to let you join in, then let it go.

My Bud Bella

Bella Thorne and I are very different people, and we have
very different views of life—but that's what makes us
come together. What I lack, she has, and whatever she
lacks, I possess. She's basically a risk-taker and doesn't
overthink anything she does, and I'm more cautious and
consider every detail, every consequence. So we feed off
each other's energy and have that perfect yin-and-yang

thing going on. We are basically our *Shake It Up* characters: what you see onscreen is a lot like we are in real life. We care about each other, we're close, we can finish each other's sentences, and we bring out the best in each other. Our personalities are a lot like Rocky's and CeCe's, too. Performing on *Shake It Up* doesn't really feel like acting—it's who we are.

We didn't know each other before *Shake It Up*. I'd seen Bella one or two times at auditions before, but we'd never had a conversation. I remember we were both up for some print ad, and she literally twirled into the room. I'd never seen someone do this before, and I was like, "Who is this girl? Where is she coming from?"

I instantly loved her. She was full of energy and confidence and spunk. Six months later, I was at the *Shake It Up* audition at a Disney studio. There were tons of girls who auditioned and sent in tapes, but the producers and casting agents narrowed it down. We had to read in front of the producers, and then they mixed and matched me with four different girls for both parts. I connected most with Rocky as a character, and when I was paired with Bella, we had instant chemistry. We knew we would groove. It was pretty funny, because when she came in, she looked familiar to me, but I couldn't put my finger on it. Then I was like, "Oh, yeah! The Twirl Girl!"

Since then, we've been together all the time—and I mean all the time, like 24/7. We'll work nine hours, then sometimes have a sleepover after. I honestly don't know how I would do this without her. It's a lot of hard work, long hours, and a lot on my shoulders. So having her to share it with me makes it so much easier, not to mention a lot of fun.

What I love the most about Bella is that she's not afraid to be herself. She'll go up to someone and just say what's on her mind, and I respect that. She's not afraid to be outside of the box. She has a lot of courage and guts, and she encourages me to let loose and take some risks when normally I wouldn't have.

One day, we got a whole bunch of boys' clothes from the set and put them on. I was wearing Roshon's clothes, and she was in Adam's clothes. We went out to the Universal CityWalk and just walked around, trying to blend in. We wanted people to think we were guys. We covered our hair in hats and hoodies so people wouldn't recognize us! It worked for a while, and we were having a blast, then a few people called us on it: "Hey, it's those Disney *Shake It Up* girls . . . in dude clothing!" They thought we were punking them. We just cracked up—it was a really silly stunt. But isn't that what friends are for? To be crazy sometimes just for the fun of it?

✳ Just Askin':
Can I stop a friendship feud?

> My BFF and I are total opposites! We can't agree on anything! What should I do?

Bella and I are opposites, and you know that opposites attract. That's why you and your bestie were drawn to each other. But here's the thing: you can't let your differences of opinion come between you. You don't always want to be arguing and turning your friendship into a firing range. My advice is to find a happy medium. Strike a compromise. She likes chocolate and you like vanilla . . . can't you guys share a swirl cone? She digs 1D and you love Pink. Can't you make a playlist with both and rock out to it? Sometimes you'll have to make sacrifices; sometimes you'll lose. But if this person is important to you, then it's worth it._____

Every relationship has to have some give-and-take. Don't focus on what your differences are. Instead, focus on how you complement each other and how you can learn from each other. Maybe she can introduce you to something you would never consider doing before! Celebrate what makes you each unique and special and how those qualities work together to make you a great team.

> When my teacher asked who spilled water on the classroom floor, my friend told on me! I had to miss recess to clean it up, and now I am so mad at her!

Put away the anger for a sec and think about why your friend did this. Was she being a tattletale to win the teacher's approval (not cool), or did she really have your best interests at heart? Was she trying to encourage you to take responsibility for your actions? Before you get upset with her, try to understand her motivation. Maybe she knows you are better than your behavior. Is it possible that she could sense your guilt and knew you wanted to fess up but didn't know how? She is likely a better friend than you think. My advice is to put it behind you and move on. Everyone makes mistakes. I'm sure your teacher will forgive you . . . and you should forgive your friend.

I've been friends with this girl since kindergarten, but now we're both crushing on the same guy. Help!

Here's what I say to this situation: "Sisters before Misters." Do not, I repeat, *do not* let a dude come between you. No matter what happens, no matter which of you girls he goes for (or neither!), someone is going to get hurt, and your friendship will suffer. Situations like this really put your bond with your bud to the test: how much does it mean to you? Crushes come and go (trust me!), but your friendship can last forever.

Avoiding Girl Drama

It can get ugly between us girls. In my fifth grade, there was a lot of talking behind one another's backs. Personally, this is one of my biggest pet peeves. If you have something to say to me, then say it to my face. Don't spread rumors or diss me when I can't defend myself. There were also lots of power struggles: one girl or group of girls trying to boss everyone around and tell us how to look and act. Like I said, ugly.

I'd like to tell you to steer clear of these drama queens, but I know that's not always possible. Often the best you can do is just be honest, respectful, and supportive of your friends. In my case, I refused to get into a "one-upping" showdown with any girl who was only interested in being popular. If someone wants to brag, be my guest. I am secure enough in myself to not go there. I also tried to never take sides, spread gossip, or treat someone in a way that I wouldn't want to be treated. Here are some other tips to avoid getting sucked into someone else's show:

♦ **Don't get stuck in the middle.** If two friends are fighting, they're of course going to ask you your opinion. Don't offer it. Someone will wind up angry at you. Let them figure it out for themselves.

♦ **Don't believe everything you hear.** Someone could easily be lying, kidding around, or making assumptions. Same goes for stuff you read online; not everyone tells the truth on Facebook or in e-mails!

♦ **Be careful whom you trust.** Don't tell your deepest secrets to just anyone. Not unless you'd like your crush broadcast over the school loudspeaker. Put your trust in girls you know can keep a secret.

◆ **Avoid girls who are controlling, critical, and just plain mean.** You know the ones I'm talking about. They may be the leaders of the pack, but their words and actions are totally toxic. You don't need that negativity around you.

Stay true to yourself. Don't let someone talk you into doing anything that feels phony or wrong. No matter what anyone says, believe in yourself.

✳ Just Askin':
Why is my bud behaving badly?

My friend went to the mall and bought the exact same outfit I was wearing! Why does she have to copy me all the time? It's annoying!

Oh, yeah . . . I've been there. Sometimes people like to jack my swag, too. Try not to feel like your friend is stealing your look. Have you ever heard the phrase "Imitation is the sincerest form of flattery"? She loves your outfit so much, she's inspired by it. If it really bugs you, tell her you'd prefer that she not wear it the same day (so you don't look like twins). Encourage her to find her own style—maybe help her go shopping for some cool new clothes. She may just be feeling insecure about her looks and needs you to give her a boost of confidence.

My friend told me my feet are huge . . . and then she said my outfit looked like a fashion emergency. I know, "sticks and stones"—but it really hurt my feelings!

Well, sometimes we say things out of anger or jealousy that we don't really mean. The best thing to do is take your friend aside and tell her how her words made you feel. Don't put her on the defensive. Just say you would like to understand where it was coming from and why she said what she said. Odds are, she'll apologize. If not, then don't stoop to her level. Just walk away.

If her behavior is turning into bullying (e.g., she's insulting you/picking on you all the time), tell someone. Involve your parents or your teacher and don't wait for them to notice. A real friend doesn't behave this way, and it's just not acceptable.

My BFF is always bragging
about all the cool stuff she has:
a flat-screen TV in her room, a
laptop, a canopy bed—now even
the new iPhone! It's getting on
my nerves—she has everything!

Is she really boasting 'bout living large, or are you just feeling a tad jealous? Jealousy is a natural feeling. You always want to be the best and have the best things. But believe me when I tell you, you're wasting your time. Instead of cataloging all the cool toys you don't have, make a list of things that are great about you. Sometimes we fail to appreciate all the awesomeness in our own lives when we're busy envying what other people have. And here's the thing: it's all just stuff. You can't buy happiness, confidence, or love. The way I see it, if you have all those things going on, then you have it pretty good, too. And who knows . . . maybe your friend wishes she could be more like you!

Breakin' Up Is Hard to Do

It happens: friends drift apart. The person you used to love to laugh and play with suddenly has new interests, a new circle of friends, and no time for you. I won't lie to you: it's hard when we lose someone who was such an important part of our life, especially if it happens out of the blue. But it's natural for friendships to fade, especially when you're in your tweens.

You're growing; you're changing. But guess what? Your BFF is doing the same. Sometimes the new, more mature you doesn't gel with the new, more mature version of your BFF. Maybe you're not in the same class or school anymore. That's okay; you can give each other some space. If the connection is strong enough, it will last between you. I've learned that really good friends find each other again and again, despite years or distance.

If the thing that's come between you is an argument or a rough patch, then it's up to you to decide what you want to do about it. I love this line from a Shakespearean sonnet about friendship: "But if the while I think on thee, dear friend, all losses are restored and sorrows end." Friends fight—but is your friendship worth fighting for? Here are some clues that it is:

- **You miss hanging out.** Even though you've been at odds or you're both too busy, you regret not having her in your life. It's so much more fun when she's around!
- **You forgot the fight.** What started this blow-out between you? If you don't know, then how important could it be?
- **You feel guilty.** There are two sides to every argument, and now you're seeing hers a little better. Maybe you're both to blame?
- **You're a great team.** The Dynamic Duo. The Two Amigas. Phineas and Ferb. That's you, and you want things to stay that way.

Ready to reconcile? There are a lot of ways to go about it. Start by reaching out to your friend: send a text or an e-mail, or simply call to say hi. Keep the initial contact short, sweet, and to the point—you're feeling out your friend to make sure she is ready to make up, too. If you haven't spoken in a while, and a conversation seems a little scary, it's nice to send a funny card in the mail to break the ice. Don't immediately try to pick up where you left off. You both may still be hanging on to some hard feelings. Your relationship needs time to heal. A simple "I'm sorry" will go a long way. Don't dwell on who's to blame or who

said/did what. You want to put all of that behind you—
forgive and forget. Focus on moving forward and the
things that make your relationship so special. Try to think
of this "pause" in your friendship as a lesson learned: if
an issue like this ever comes up again between you, you'll
know how to deal with it better.

✳ Just Askin':
How do I say farewell to a friend?

My bestie is moving at the end of the summer
... and I'm never gonna see her again! I feel
awful. What can I do?

I've been through this and I completely understand. I
moved from my hometown of Oakland to L.A., where
I had no friends. I didn't know anyone, and I really
missed the gang I left behind. The thing to do is stay
connected, and luckily, there are many ways to keep connected nowadays. Pick up the phone and call; send a text
or an e-mail; or video-chat each other. I know it's not the
same thing as going to your friend's house every day after

school, but it can make the distance between you feel so much more manageable.

I had a best friend who moved to Florida in fourth grade, and I was completely devastated. We drifted apart for a while, thanks to our busy lives, but last year, we reconnected. We stayed up all night talking, and it was like we had never said good-bye. We picked up right where we left off. If you have a true friendship, it will last. It's up to you guys to find creative and fun ways to reach out to each other. I know you can do it.

My friend is giving me the cold shoulder in school. When I try to call her or talk to her, she just ignores me or says I'm being a stalker!

If your friend doesn't want to talk over whatever it is that's come between you, then it may be time to call it quits with your relationship. Basically, it's her problem, not yours. You have the right to expect a friend to be there for you, and she's clearly not doing her job. Whatever the reason for the falling-out, I say move on. Why waste your time on someone who doesn't appreciate you when you can find a new friend who's happy to have you around?

DIY: Throw a Super Slumber Party

There is nothing quite like a night in with the girls!

- **Theme it.** Some great ones are spa treatments (give everyone mani/pedis and face masks), makeovers (do everyone's makeup and hair), horror movies (creepy flick marathon and ghost stories!), bake-overs (bake and decorate cupcakes and cookies), and style swaps (everyone brings clothes to swap and model).

- **Create a keepsake.** It's fun to decorate white pillowcases with fabric markers (a cool souvenir) or give everyone tees or tanks to autograph. I'm also a big fan of making friendship bracelets, necklaces, earrings, and even key chains to swap and share.

- **Stock up on snacks.** Make sure you have lots of yummy munchies for staying up till midnight (or sunrise!). I love this recipe for ultimate s'mores pizza!

Ultimate S'mores Pizza

You'll need:

    1 12" ready-made pizza dough
    1 cup crumbled graham crackers
    1 cup semisweet chocolate chips or chunks
    2 cups mini marshmallows

Heat the oven to 350°F. Place pizza dough on a greased cookie sheet and bake for five minutes. Remove from oven and top with graham cracker crumbs, chocolate chips, and marshmallows, layering the ingredients so you get a nice mix. Return to oven for five minutes until marshmallows are golden brown on top and the chocolate is melted. Dig in!

To Sum It Up:

Surround yourself with friends who like you for who you are. You want a group you can lean on when the going gets tough. True friends are loyal, respectful, and worthy of your trust. Anyone else . . . *hasta la vista*!

Chapter 2

School Days

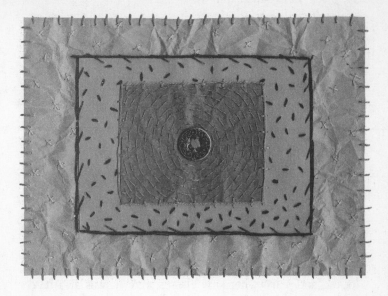

When it came to my first day of school

every year, I was always a jumble of feelings. Part of me was totally psyched: I couldn't wait to rock a hot new outfit I'd picked out. I was eager to see which kids were in my class and to find out what everyone did over the summer. But there was another part of me that was also a little nervous: what if my teacher was really strict? What if my classes were super-hard? What if I forgot my multiplication tables? What if no one sat with me at lunch? And on and on . . .

If you're dreading that first day, you're not alone. Everyone feels this way because there's a lot on the line. Each new school year is a new beginning. The calm, safe, secure feeling you left behind in June has now been replaced with uncertainty and butterflies.

For me, the most stressful first day was the start of my new school, the Oakland School of the Arts, in 2008. They were still building our school, so classes were held in portable units, and everyone from sixth-graders to twelfth-graders was pushing past one another in the halls. It was confusing and intimidating! It was my first time having a schedule and having to bounce from class to class. I was worried I'd be late or I'd walk into the wrong room. I remember wondering how I would make friends, figure out how to open my locker, and learn where my classes were. It was also hard going from being an all-knowing "senior" in elementary school to a clueless "freshman" in middle school. Suddenly, I was at the bottom of the ladder again!

My advice to you is to keep calm and don't panic, no matter what grade you're entering. Try to focus on the positive ("I can totally reinvent myself and my style!") instead of the negative ("What if no one likes me?"). Don't let your nerves get the best of you. Remind yourself that you've done this successfully several times before—this isn't your first day in pre-K. You know pretty much what's expected of you, how the day will go, and what the obstacles might be. Take a deep breath, smile big, and step through those front doors with confidence!

First-day Fear-busters

Here's how to defuse your anxiety before it even has a chance to rattle you!

"I'm worried I'll get lost in the halls/ on campus." Get your hands on a school map (from the registration office or online) so you can be confident you are heading in the right direction. You also can ask other students for directions; there's no shame in it. It's a great way to introduce yourself and maybe make a new friend, too.

"I know I'll be late!" Use the night before the first day to prep. Lay out your outfit; pack your backpack with all your supplies; choose your shoes and accessories. That way, when you wake up, you'll be ready to rock!

"The first day always stinks." Ditch that attitude. Picture yourself having a great time. This is called creative visualization, and I swear it works wonders! Performers and pro athletes use it all the time. If you can see it, you can be it!

"I'm scared no one will talk to me." Call some friends from last year and catch up either over the phone or in person. Reconnect before the first day, so you'll have that bond. If you're totally new to a school, ask the administration if you can meet or chat with a kid in your grade and get the scoop over the summer. That way, you won't be a total stranger; you'll know someone already.

"I forgot everything I learned last year!" Then go back over your old notes, quiz yourself, review, and refresh your memory. Apps are a great way to test yourself on math, vocabulary, even science facts—and it doesn't feel like homework if you're "playing" them on your phone or tablet.

"I am totally freaking out!" Breathe. Meditate. Dance it out. Do whatever you need to do to take your mind off your nerves. I like to stand in front of a mirror and actually rehearse my "lines"—what I will say when I run into people or how I will greet my peers and teachers. It's a great way to get control and calm yourself down.

✳ Just Askin':
How can I keep my cool?

I am starting a new school this year, and I met a girl who goes there. She told me sixth grade was so hard, she almost failed! Now I'm freaking . . .

Everyone is different—so please don't go by what your new friend might have told you about her experiences. Just because she had a tough time in class doesn't mean you will. That said, if you do find that you're falling behind in your studies, speak up. Ask your teachers or your parents to get you some extra help. Approach your new school with a great attitude ("I will do the very best I can!"), and you'll be off to a great start.

I keep having these nightmares about middle school! I wake up in a cold sweat. Why can't I just stay in fifth grade forever?

Unless you're Peter Pan, you gotta grow up sometime. Kids deal with nerves in different ways. Trouble sleeping is one of them; hair twirling, nail biting, and foot tapping are some others. I went through a time when I was very afraid of failing school. I've always gotten good grades, but for some reason, my confidence was taking a nosedive. I would have nightmares about schoolwork and tests, and I was a nervous wreck all the time. I confided in my parents and my teachers, and they helped me. I also told myself that my fear wasn't making me any smarter or preventing me from tanking on a test. What did help was writing my fears down on a piece of paper. Just putting them out there made them feel easier to tackle. Make a list and try to sort out what's eating you. What can you do to fix it? Take it one step at a time, and tell yourself that this time next year, it will all be in the past. You'll be an experienced middle schooler, and you wouldn't want it any other way.

Exam Anxiety

Taking a test makes you feel:
- ◉ nervous
- ○ queasy
- ○ petrified
- ○ all of the above.

If you chose any of these, welcome to the club! I feel your pain! Just seeing those multiple-choice questions made me feel shaky and sweaty. My teachers would have to take me out in the hallway and tell me, "Calm down, Zendaya. Take a deep breath." I would panic for no reason. Especially in earth science—that's just not my calling. One mention of compost or earthworms and I was a wreck.

What I learned (after several embarrassing moments pre-exam) is that this behavior does nothing to improve my test scores. What does help is developing good study habits. I know your teachers tell you that all the time, but it's true. If you can get a grip on what you need to learn and commit it to your memory in an efficient, effective way—you're home free.

SUPER STUDY TIPS

✓ **Start with a good attitude.** If you approach your upcoming test thinking you're going to fail, chances are that you will. Don't dwell on how you did in the past. This is a new opportunity to both prove and improve yourself.

✓ **Don't compare yourself to others.** If your BFF tells you, "I don't have to study; I know it all already," then good for her. She may be an ace at algebra. You do what's best for you and focus on what you need to know.

✓ **Choose a quiet study spot that's free from distractions.** If your bro is playing video games while you're trying to study, you are not going to absorb anything. Stay away from TV, radio, computers, phones—anything that might pull your attention away from your textbooks.

✓ **Take a break.** Don't try to force facts into your brain for hours on end. Set a reasonable time limit to study, then get up, stretch, have a snack, etc. Every hour or so, give yourself five to ten minutes of downtime before you hit the books again.

✓ **Put it on paper and rewrite your notes.** I am the flash card queen! Somehow, when I scribble down facts again, it helps me understand them better—and they sink in. Your brain remembers putting them down on paper! Review the notes you've taken from your textbook and class, then make yourself a study sheet or card that highlights the most important facts for your test.

✓ **Play memory games**—letters that stand for things (e.g., ROYGBIV for the order of colors in a rainbow: red, orange, yellow, green, blue, indigo, violet); little rhymes or songs. This is a lot of fun to do with a friend! Try rockin' out to a rap of the Preamble to the Constitution ("We the peeps, in order to form a more perfect union . . . Break it down now!"). Or when you have a biology test, the "the shinbone's connected to the knee bone" tune can help you label a tough diagram. Or the rhyme "I before e, except after c" can be the key to acing your spelling quiz. Inventing fun ways to remember facts will help prevent brain freeze.

✓ **Get enough z's.** Try to get at least eight hours of sleep the night before any test. Your body and your brain need time to recharge their batteries. It's also a great idea to eat a good breakfast for extra brain fuel.

✓ **Learn something.** Don't just memorize facts or formulas and forget them the minute the test is over. Use your study time to commit these facts to your long-term memory. Think about how you can apply them in practical ways in your life (like, can percentages help you calculate how much that cute bag is on sale?). This is what makes a good student rather than a good test taker.

✳ Just Askin':
Truth be told

> I failed my pre-algebra quiz even though I studied, and I'm scared to tell my parents. They're gonna be so mad!

I think your parents will respect you more if you actually go to them and tell the truth. I would say, "Look, guys, I studied really hard, and it just didn't work out. I tried my best." As long as you emphasize the fact that you gave it a hundred percent, they will understand it was not your fault. Maybe it has something to do with the way you're learning it, and a teacher or tutor can help. I would not hide your F from your folks. You want their help and support, not their distrust.

> My BFF asked me to write a book report for her. I feel like it's cheating, but I'm afraid if I say no, she won't be my friend anymore.

You're right; it *is* cheating. If your teacher found out,

you'd both be in huge trouble, maybe even suspended. Tell your bestie that she has to do her own homework; you're not comfortable doing it for her. It's dishonest and it's not helping her learn anything. Offer to help her brainstorm and better understand the book. But no way should you do her work for her—even if she begs, pleads, or threatens. If she doesn't understand that—or says she won't be your friend anymore—then she wasn't your friend in the first place.

How to Be an A+ Student

Wanna win your teacher's approval? Here are some great pointers!

- **Be on time.** Tardiness is the quickest way to make your teachers see red. They view it as laziness and lack of respect for the learning process. If you have a teacher who's especially tough, then get to class early and be eager to learn!
- **Lend a hand.** Whenever your teacher needs books carried, pencils sharpened, a memo brought to the principal's office, you're just the person for the job. Volunteer for every task. Even if your

teacher doesn't thank you, she'll notice your helpfulness.

◆ **Come prepared.** That means having all your supplies at hand (no excuses!) and your homework done. If you have a long-term assignment, then don't leave it to the last minute. Budget your time and make sure you turn it in on the date it's due (or early if you can manage!).

◆ **Pay attention.** Even if the rest of the class is goofing off/talking loudly, give your teacher the utmost respect she deserves.

Shake Off Your Shyness

I'm a talker—my *Shake It Up* cast mates will tell you I rarely zip my lips even when the director calls, "Quiet on the set!" So I know it's hard to believe I was ever painfully shy. Believe it! When I was in elementary school, I never raised my hand in class, and I hated giving oral reports in front of people. Weird, I know—I stand onstage all the time now in front of a live audience, and I sing to crowds of thousands. But back then, I didn't have the same confidence. Everything made me feel self-conscious. I just wanted to shrink and hide.

Shyness may be something you're born with, but I am living proof that you can conquer it. I remember very clearly how it feels: sometimes it's a timidness—as in, I knew the answer in class but I just couldn't summon the courage to say it. Other times, it's pretty paralyzing—like the whole world was staring and waiting for me to do something stupid. Shyness is being uncomfortable in a social situation—and that's what school is all about. Shy people have a hard time making eye contact, sticking up for themselves, even making friends. I didn't like being shy, and I felt like it held me back. My mom and dad tried to encourage me not to clam up in front of a crowd. In my performing-arts school, you had to get up in front of the class and act. I wanted a good grade, so I had no choice! After a while, it became second nature to me. But in the beginning, I had to summon the courage to stand up and speak up. Here are some helpful tips to shake off your shyness:

Change your mind. Consider what you're saying to yourself when you're feeling shy. Is it "I can't do this" or "I might embarrass myself"? Try to replace those thoughts with more positive ones: "I can do this!" and "I'm going to be awesome!"

Be a star at something. Everyone has talents and things that make them special. Do them and see your self-confidence soar. It's important to work on feeling good about your abilities. My parents had me do a lot of sports when I was really little so that I could become more confident. I didn't want to do them, and I was really more into just being with my friends, but they said I had to do something active and try it for just one season. So I did. I never really liked sports all that much, but it helped me get over being shy.

Then I discovered dance! I joined Future Shock Oakland when I was eight, and I wasn't very good at all. I had a hard time keeping up and learning the dance moves with all the older kids, but slowly I got better and better and developed good friendships. In fact, the kids I met back then are still my best friends now, and are dancing with me on my "Swag It Out" tour. I can sometimes still be shy when I don't know people, but I like to think of it more as being laid-back rather than timid. That's just who I am!

Build your supporting cast. Surround yourself with people who cheer you on and bring out the best in you. If you feel like you have people rooting for you, you'll be able to do so much more.

Smile and look people in the eye. Even if you say nothing, this is a great way to interact. You'll find that people will react warmly toward you—and that makes it so much easier to strike up a conversation.

Hold your head high. When you're shy, you tend to slump. Practice confident body language: shoulders back, chin up!

School on the Set

When you're a kid actor, you have to go to school on-set—that's the child labor law according to the State of California. Usually, I'm in class for five hours a day, which is a lot when you have rehearsals and shooting as well. Because we're both in high school, Bella and I share a teacher, Monique Fisher, and she's amazing. I get homework; I take tests; I write five-page essays. I study everything from biology and algebra to English, history, and Spanish. I even have to take P.E.! I have to maintain satisfactory grades or I won't be allowed to work on *Shake It Up*—so that's a lot of pressure. I'll graduate when I'm eighteen, just like any high-school kid—and I really want to go to college. I do miss the social aspect of being in a regular school, but I love the individual attention I get from my teacher. I don't have to raise my hand, but it's also hard to pass a note to Bella and not get caught!

Homework Overload!

After spending the entire day straining your brain to learn facts and figures, all you want to do is chill. So why are your teachers piling on the homework? Here's the thing: homework is a review of what you've studied in school. Some teachers assign more than others, but the goal is the same: homework reinforces the concepts covered in class and makes sure you know how to apply them.

In elementary school, you were probably doing no more than forty-five minutes to an hour each night (with the occasional days off for good behavior!). You might have even done it with pretty colored pencils or markers (I used to like to illustrate my writing assignments!). But when you're a tween, homework can take more than two hours a night, and it's pretty serious business. It has to be neat; it has to be complete. I don't know about you, but I am the queen of erasing!

For me, homework always comes first, even before my "day job" on *Shake It Up*. Education is my top priority, so I will study and get my reports done for school before I hit my script and start memorizing Rocky's lines. I don't love homework, but I am not a homework hater, either. I tell myself that this is my chance to work independently and show how mature and responsible I can be. The smarter you are, the more you can handle. So bring it on. . . .

Homework Helpers

- **Keep a planner with all your important due dates in it:** book reports, tests, social studies dioramas, etc. Check it every day to make sure you're on track. If you can tackle something ahead of time, do it!

- **Have a specific time every day that you set aside for homework.** If you need to give your brain a brief break after school, then make your "homework hour" late afternoon/early evening.

- **Reserve a quiet spot to do your homework where there are no distractions** (e.g., TV, e-mail, phone, video games). I like to curl up on the couch in my dressing room or on my bed at home.

- **Don't put it off.** Procrastinating will only make you more anxious. Never leave any assignment to the last minute.

- **Break it up.** If you have a huge pile of work you need to do tonight, then divide it into smaller piles. Work on one thing at a time. Put away each assignment as you finish it, and your mountain will get smaller and feel less scary.

- **If you don't understand how to do part of your homework, don't skip it or leave it to another day.** Call a friend, ask a sibling or parent, or research it online. If you still don't have a solution, then go to your teacher first thing in the a.m. and ask for a further explanation.

✳ Just Askin':
Extra help

> I'm doing really badly in math, and my parents got me a tutor. I am so embarrassed—what if my friends make fun of me or call me stupid?

You're not dumb for needing a tutor. In fact, you're really smart to speak up about not understanding a subject. Everyone needs a little extra help now and then. Sometimes I have to stop my teacher and go, "Wait a sec. I don't get it. Can you do that again?" I really needed help with my multiplication facts once, and I spent a day with my grandma working on them. She would quiz me by posting equations and answers all over the kitchen. So she'd say, "What's six times four?" and I'd look at the microwave and there would be a sign that said 24. Does that mean I'm dumb? I'd better not hear you say that! Unless you're a total brainiac, you're not going to understand everything instantly. People learn at different speeds. If your parents are concerned and think you need extra help, then take it. Who wouldn't want insurance that they'll rock their next math test? As for your friends, they will probably be coming to you soon for homework help!

To Sum It Up:

Toto, we're not in Kansas anymore! Middle school is a lot tougher than elementary school when it comes to classes, homework, and teachers. Be proud that more is expected of you (because you can do it!), and set yourself up with smart study habits.

Chapter 3

Swag It Out!

I am kind of a fashion chameleon—my look is always changing, which I think is a really good thing when you're a tween. You should be trying out new styles; you should be discovering what makes you look and feel good. Unless your school has a dress code (and even then you can have lots of fun on weekends and after school!), I say, go for it! Experiment with your outfits every day.

Sometimes my outfits win rave reviews, and other times they get some pretty puzzled looks. But I don't care either way. For me, fashion is about being inventive and creative; it's playing with color, texture, pattern, and cut, and mixing them up to achieve something fresh, new, and exciting. It's kind of like my own *Project Runway* every day! My fashion philosophy is simple: Be who you are!

Three things really affect what I wear:

My mood. Seriously, you can tell when I'm tired because my outfit choices are less inspired! When I'm full of energy, I pull out all the stops. But I also use fashion to lift me up on days when I could use a boost. A bright shirt or a funky hat just makes me smile!

My destination. My look depends on where I'm going. For example, on the red carpet, sometimes I like to rock classic old-Hollywood style. I mean, come on— it's the red carpet! So I have fun with it: I wear elegant dresses, a soft wave in my hair, and eyeliner to give me that 1940s cat-eye. Other times, I might wear sequins and skinny jeans with a graphic tee and boots—stuff that's cool and funky but not over the top. But on my personal time, my look is way different. I guess you could call it "urban hipster." I like wearing harem pants and fun prints, and I mix and match stuff that kind of clashes. I also love to wear cool boots—they make me walk tall (literally—and that gives me a confidence boost!)—and all kinds of sneakers.

My company. Who I'm hanging with is another big factor. When it's just my friends, I dress more casual and comfy. I'm chill with my friends, so there's no need to dress to impress. But if I'm going to a meeting or an interview, I step it up a notch. I'll choose clothes that give me confidence. I want to be taken seriously!

My style has changed so much since elementary school! Back then, I was a tomboy. Basically, I wore khaki cargo shorts from the boys' section and big sweatshirts and sneakers. My next phase was Abercrombie: it was seriously all I wanted to wear. If it didn't have "A&F" on it, I wasn't buying it. Next came my "blouse and bun" look: a shirt, jeans, and some little boots, and my hair pinned up and rolled back on each side. I guess it made me feel more grown-up to wear my hair up and swap my tees for something more tailored.

When I got to middle school, I realized I was tired of wearing what was "in" or "trendy." I wanted to set my own trends! I wanted to take my look and "Zendaya-fy" it! I pretty much knew what styles flattered me and made me feel cool and confident. "But Z," you say, "how do I find *my* style?" So glad you asked!

☞ What's My Style Personality?

Time for a pop quiz—but this one is fun and easy, I promise! I want you to answer the following questions, then check your results. Once you have your style personality, you're ready to start dressing to show it off.

My favorite place to shop is:
- a. a costume store
- b. the trendiest store
- c. J. Crew
- d. a sporting-goods store

My friends would describe me as:
- a. Lady Gaga's twin
- b. ahead of the trends
- c. polite and well-mannered
- d. a tomboy

I spend most of my time:

   a. in the spotlight
   b. reading style magazines
   c. at the library
   d. on a team

One day, I'd like to:

   a. perform on Broadway
   b. win *Project Runway*
   c. have tea at Buckingham Palace
   d. win a sports award

If I had $100, I'd buy:

   a. a sparkly tee
   b. a stylish bag
   c. a delicate necklace
   d. a pair of high-end sneakers

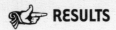 **RESULTS**

You answered mostly A's: Your style is DRAMATIC. If it sparkles and shines, it probably has your name on it. Why? Because you love to stand out in a crowd! You can (and should!) be bold with your fashion choices—don't shy away from bright color, big patterns, or even (gulp!) tops and bottoms that clash. If there is anyone who can pull it off, it's you. To avoid accidentally overdoing it, you may want to choose one or two pieces that make a statement and let the rest of your outfit be the supporting cast.

You answered mostly B's: Your style is FASHIONISTA. Girlfriend, fashion is your passion, and you take your cues from the runway and the red carpet. You love to shop till you drop (my kind of girl!) and would save every cent of your allowance to score that super-cute bag you saw in your favorite magazine. What can you do to give the looks you love your own brand of unique chic? Accessorizing is a fashionista's key to coolness. Stock up on inexpensive accessories—they can really transform your outfit from average to awesome. My thing is shoes. My closet is filled with everything from

Me and the lovely lady who brought me into this world—a.k.a. my mommy!

Howdy! A lil' bit a modeling for y'all!

Me and the only person who actually may know me better than I know myself . . . my big niece, Zink.

Weeerrrrk, baby me!
Afro-swag!

Me and Zink
BAALLIIINNNN'!

Beast Mode on the
soccer field!

First day of second grade . . .
someone was feelin' themselves!

Daddy's girl!

Me and my Poppi!

Me and my little baby, Midnight, or should I say my BIG baby!

Me and my BFF Dom were too cute for Halloween!

Me and mommy

Playing Little Ti Moune in *Once on This Island*

Hey! It's J-Lo, Alicia Keys, and Mariah! SMH!!

The fam bam!

Epic water-skiing!

Trip to the Golden Gate

Dad couldn't handle
water-skiing . . .
only for us pros! JK

Camping with Mom's class

His name was Austin!

Me and my little cuzzo's . . . Whit and Jess

Me and my little niece, Berky . . . she's just so cute, it's ridiculous!

Hot stuff! LOL

This might be the most recent picture of me and my mom . . . she never lets me take pictures of her (she's a little camera shy).

combat boots to heels to sneakers—you name it!
So I will take an outfit and give it a twist by wearing funky footwear.

You answered mostly C's: Your style is CLASSIC. Ladylike and timeless is the look you love. Pretty and polished are your style mantras, so you should look for clothes that are soft, tailored, and elegant. Shop for staples like a crisp white shirt or a polished blazer, and ask your mom if you can pretty-please borrow her cashmere sweater. Find a few perf pieces that you can mix and match, and don delicate details (a pretty scarf, a ribbon headband, sparkly stud earrings, shiny patent-leather ballet slippers) to dress them up.

You answered mostly D's: Your style is SPORTY. Girly-girl looks? Not your thing! You are all about comfy clothes that let you move and groove. I used to rock the tomboy look, too. Balance your tops and bottoms so they work together—like a long and loose tunic over some stretchy leggings. Graphic tees with your fave team's logo are ultra cool; and you can never go wrong with a pair of jeans or yoga pants and some fun kicks. Why not start a sneaker collection? I did!

Confessions of a Shopaholic

Shopping is something I can do anytime—I don't need a reason. If one of my friends suggests hitting the stores, I have one foot out the door already. Yes, I confess, I am a natural-born shopper—and proud of it! I especially love to browse for bargains, and when there's a "Sale" sign in the window, it calls to me. But trust me when I tell you it's not just about combing the racks. There is a science to being a great shopper!

Bring along a trusted fashion adviser. You want someone who has a good eye, keen fashion sense, and can be totally, one-hundred-percent honest with you. In my case, that person is my dad. My mom tells me everything looks beautiful on me (she's my mom—of course she thinks that!). But Dad tells it like it is. I'll put together an outfit and ask him what he thinks of it. Sometimes, he gives me that "face." He kind of wrinkles up his nose and shakes his head. That's when I take a good, hard look in the mirror to see if he's right. Most of the time, he is! And I'll rethink it or switch something around. It's a good idea to have a friend, sibling, or parent with you if you're thinking about buying something. And it's pretty fun to have an audience when you're trying on clothes, don't you think?

Don't budge on your budget. Seriously, this is how a lot of girls get into trouble. If you know you only have $30 to spend on an outfit for your BFF's b'day bash, try not to spend it all on one item. Ask yourself if it's really worth it. Could you find a similar look somewhere else for less? I give myself props for being able to find inexpensive separates and pull them together into a runway-ready look. It's fun to be creative, and it's mature and responsible to set financial limits for yourself.

Check your look from all angles. This is what three-way mirrors in dressing rooms are for! I always do a spin, then a bend and a stretch. How does the outfit feel and look when I stand, sit, reach, etc. Does the waist creep down or up? Does the top ride up? Is it still comfortable when I sit down? I also like to make sure my clothes aren't going to give me any surprises—like suddenly turning see-through when I step into the light. Smart shoppers scope out their outfits with a critical eye!

Keep the receipt. How many times have you come home with a shirt in a shopping bag, only to discover you could have used one size bigger/smaller? The lesson learned here: always hang on to the receipt. Some stores won't even let you exchange an item unless you have one. I tuck mine in a special section of my wallet so I never have to hunt for it in the bottom of my bag.

Never shop in a hurry. I can't stress this enough. If you're pressed for time, don't make a purchase. Grab-and-go is not a good fashion strategy—you'll always regret it later. Leave yourself enough time at a store to try things on, compare sizes, cuts, and colors, and find the perfect accessories. Same goes for shopping when you're tired or hungry. You can't make smart choices unless you're feeling your best!

Scope out a new store. I don't like to find myself in a fashion rut. Even if I have some favorite boutiques and brands, I think it's fun and exciting to shop somewhere I've never tried before. I think of it as a style scavenger hunt! You never know what treasures could be lurking inside the boys' department or a thrift shop! Sometimes I get ideas from the outfits the stylists choose for us on *Shake It Up*. I'll say, "Ooooh, I like this! Where's it from?" Then I'll make a mental note to check it out online or in the mall. When it comes to style, open-minded is my middle name. (Actually, it's Maree!)

Don't buy it just because it's on sale. Tempting as it may be, if that seventy-percent-off sweater doesn't look right on you, return it to the rack! How much of a bargain will it be if you never wear it? Only buy what you love.

Trends are always changing. So it's not a great

idea to spend a huge amount on an item that's "in" today and gone tomorrow. If you want to buy a few fun pieces to jazz up your look, go for it. Just be mindful of how you divvy up your dollars. Spend the most on things that have staying power, like a fab denim jacket, a short black skirt, or a cute pair of boots. None of the above will ever go out of style, so you'll get your money's worth.

*Just Askin':
Rockin' Rocky's look

I just love how Rocky Blue dresses on <u>Shake It Up</u>. How do I get that look?

I get asked this question A LOT. Rocky really is quite the fashion-forward girl! Seriously, I love to dress for my role. I also like that the stylists on the show ask my opinion about the clothes. Sometimes I'll say, "That's a little too dark or dull for Rocky," and they respect that. I feel like I know her inside and out by now!

In a lot of ways, Rocky's style is similar to my own— we have a lot of the same basic pieces. But Rocky is a little more girly than I am. I might take one of her cute, ruffly skirts and add tights and combat boots and a leather jacket, and she might do it with something a little softer, like a cropped sweater and sneakers.

The key to Rocky's look is really mixing things up. Don't go for the predictable pairing. Mix patterns, shapes, textures, and colors. Wear a casual shoe style (like a sneaker or a boot) with a more formal skirt. There are so many possibilities! This shopping list should help you build a "Rocky-esque" wardrobe—just remember to make it your own!

Shopping list:

- ✓ colorful tights and leggings
- ✓ boots
- ✓ crop/off-the-shoulder tops
- ✓ mix-and-match patterns (stripes, plaids, polka dots, florals)
- ✓ flowy short skirts
- ✓ cropped denim jackets and vests
- ✓ shrugs and short cardigans
- ✓ fun graphic tops
- ✓ high-top sneakers
- ✓ belts
- ✓ long necklaces

Style File: Ten Wardrobe Must-Haves

Your style is what sets you apart, but every girl needs somewhere to start and some basics to build on. If you have these ten items, you can't go wrong!

- **Simple fitted jeans.** You can dress them up, you can dress them down. A dark wash is very versatile and flattering.

- **A great pair of boots.** Whether they're combat, cowboy, or equestrian, you can pretty much wear them with everything in your closet. A good, solid pair will be able to take whatever you dish out.

- **A classic white tee or tank top.** I wear these under everything, from a cute blazer to a funky vest. It's my go-to top when I have no clue what to pair with a bottom. It will never let you down! If you're artsy, you can also embellish one with an appliqué, beading around the neck, or a fabric bow. It's all in the details!

- **A bold accessory.** I really love chunky, beaded necklaces and bracelets and long chains. I layer them when I need to give my outfit some more "oomph." I also always wear a big watch. It's my

statement piece, and it speaks for itself. I put it on
and BAM! Instant dress to impress!

♦ **A chic sweater.** Look for a basic cotton cardigan
in a neutral color (black, white, navy) that you can
layer over everything from a tee to a sundress. I like
mine to have a little swing to it when I walk.

♦ **A bag that holds everything.** I like mine
to have some color, texture, or detail—it jazzes
up whatever I'm wearing. I also recommend
finding one with lots of pockets to help keep you
organized. I load my purse up! I always have
my earphones, my script, my phone, lip gloss,
sunglasses, and tons of gum (gotta keep it minty)!

♦ **A cool pair of shorts.** These are as versatile as a
skirt and so comfortable. Whether they're printed,
metallic, or beaded, you can pair them with a white
tee and feel dressed up!

♦ **A hot pair of heels.** Not too high—you don't
want to hurt yourself! I think a wedge or a slight
platform is comfy and easy to walk around in.
Skinny heels hurt! I also love peep toes—I think
they're fun, and I like to show off a pretty pedi!

♦ **A denim jacket.** Again, this goes with anything
you have in your closet, from a cute sundress to
cargo pants. I like mine cropped and fitted. Sew on

patches, crystals, or piping around the collar and
cuffs to give it your own style spin.

♦ **A cute dress.** Easy to pull on (zip up and zip out
the door!) and always stylish, whether you wear it
to school or a birthday party. You can't go wrong
with a simple sheath in a bright, cheery color
(yellow, green, blue . . . go for it!). I also love bold
prints—they just make me feel happy. For hotter
days, a long, flowy maxi dress is so effortlessly
gorge!

✳Just Askin':
Bra advice

My mom thinks it's time for me
to get a training bra, but I am
really worried that my friends will
make fun of me in the locker room!

Do not stress out about this! If someone says something
negative to you, just remind them, "Hey, we're girls. We
all have to wear 'em sometime!" A training bra is a great

way to start because it's soft and comfy and offers a little coverage where you need it (like under a thin tee). There are many that don't even look like bras; some resemble a stretchy cropped tank. You are so lucky that your mom came to you and suggested it. I was actually really nervous, and I didn't know how to ask my mom to buy me one! I was like, "Hey, Mom, this is kind of awkward, but I think it's a good time to go bra shopping . . . " She was totally down for it and made me feel more at ease.

Blast from the Past: Vintage Shopping

I love vintage—it's like walking around wearing history. My stylist actually owns a vintage store, and he finds all this crazy, cool stuff. Some of the clothes are over fifty years old—like the dress I wore to the Teen Choice Awards in 2012. It was a 1950s white tulle prom dress, and I felt so elegant and special in it. I paired it with a leather vest, a belt, and hot-pink heels to give it some extra funk.

Buying vintage takes a little legwork. You literally have to hunt through racks of random pieces at thrift stores, garage sales, and flea markets to find what you're looking for—but it's worth it! Just know that vintage clothing should be checked for stains, rips, pulls, pilling, missing buttons, stuck zippers, broken clasps, etc. If you do find something you love that's damaged, ask how and if it can be fixed. The beauty of vintage is that you can also haggle on the price, especially if the piece is flawed.

Heel Appeal

I have had a fascination with high heels since I was a little girl. I liked to try my mom's on and stomp around the house. There is nothing that makes me feel quite as glam. You might be buying your first pair now for a special occasion, and you want to make sure a) the shoes fit and b) you won't break your neck in them. Here are my tips to avoid blisters and trips!

- **Start small.** For your first pair, try a one- or two-inch heel. Once you master these, you can move on to higher ones.
- **Test them out.** Do not wear your heels somewhere straight out of the box! You need to break them in. I walk around my house or dressing room in them (as silly as I look, it works!) for a day or two. Sometimes I look a little funny: strappy sandals don't exactly go with sweats! But a girl's

gotta do what a girl's gotta do! If they're stiff, wear
them with socks to soften and stretch them a bit.
I try them walking up and down stairs or pacing
quickly and then slowly. If you're worried about
slipping, you can get some nonslip grip pads for the
soles to provide some traction.

◆ **Pad where it hurts.** Wherever you feel pressure
or rubbing, you can apply a protective cushion.
These come in lots of materials, from gel pads for
the balls of your feet to soft heel guards you stick
inside your shoes.

◆ **Walk carefully.** When you feel wobbly, you
might be tempted to stomp your whole foot down
at once. But walking heel first, followed by toe,
gives you more balance. Also, walk more slowly
and take shorter steps. Until you're a pro at this,
don't run!

Bling It Up!

I am a gold girl. And silver. And rhinestones. Heck, there
isn't anything sparkly and shiny that I would turn down!
But I do believe that sometimes less is more when it
comes to jewelry. It really depends on the outfit. If your

clothes are bold and embellished, then there's no need to add accessory bling. You want your jewelry to complement—not compete with—your look.

I like to mix metallics and different types and lengths of beaded necklaces. I kind of make my own rules when it comes to layering; I just pile on a few pieces that seem to work well together and add a little something to my outfit. Whatever I'm feelin', I just go with it. Maybe it's not what you would choose, and that's okay! Do your own thing with your bling! A lot of tween girls like personalized jewelry like a charm bracelet, a monogram necklace, or a locket. I love any and all of the above because they speak to who you are. Whatever jewelry you choose, make sure to take good care of it. Store it in a jewelry box, or a bag, or in an individual pouch so that the chains don't get tangled and tarnished.

DIY: Make an Earring Holder!

If you've got a collection of studs, hoops, and dangles like I do, it's fun to display it in a pretty earring keeper designed by you!

✳ ❀ ✳ ❀ ✳ ❀ ✳ ❀ ✳ ❀ ✳ ❀ ✳

You'll need:

A mesh cooking splatter screen (you can find them in a hardware store, a dollar store, or a cooking supply store)

Burlap fabric (approx. 1 yard)

Hot glue/glue gun

Decorative ribbon (approx. 1 yard)

Plastic jewels or buttons

1. Lay the screen on top of the burlap and trace the size of the circle. Cut the burlap out slightly larger than the circle, so you have some room to tuck and glue it.
2. Pull tightly around the edges of the frame and tuck the burlap under, gluing it in place.
3. Decorate the edges of the screen with pretty ribbon glued in place.

4. Decorate the handle, winding the ribbon around it and tying the ribbon in a bow.
5. Beautify your earring holder by gluing studs, buttons, or jewels in a pretty pattern around the edge of the screen.
6. Push the posts of your earrings through the burlap and the screen.
7. Hang your new earring holder on the wall!

✳ Just Askin':
Style veto

My parents refuse to let me get my ears pierced till I'm thirteen! All my friends have already had it done, and I am the only one who doesn't get to wear cute earrings!

I hear ya—but your parents are your parents, and you have to play by their rules. Have you asked them why they feel this way? Is there any way you can arrive at a compromise? In the meantime, I say fake it till you make it! You can find all sorts of cute clip-on, stick-on, and magnet earrings that look as good as the real thing. I also think ear cuffs are cool—they just cling around the top part of your ear. You'll look great, and your parents won't be angry. Win-win!

Our school has a dress code. We always have to wear khaki skirts and white shirts. I hate it! What can I do to look cooler?

Your school has rules—and you have to abide by them. So

I don't suggest rebelling or trying to get away with wearing something that's not in the school handbook. That said, maybe there is some wiggle room. Are you allowed to wear cool tights or socks? These can add instant "oomph" to an outfit. Or how about cute headbands or barrettes? What about outerwear—can your coat, sweater, or hoodie add some zip? What about a fun scarf? And don't overlook your hairdo—this can provide instant style. Switch it up: one day wear a braid; one day curl it; one day slick it straight. If there are no specific guidelines about backpacks or totes, then jazz yours up with pins, buttons, ribbons, patches—anything that adds personality and helps you stand out from the crowd.

Hit the Road—with Style!

I travel a lot—coast to coast and around the globe. I've been everywhere, from NYC and Phoenix to Paris, London, and Dubai, between promoting *Shake It Up* and doing my concerts. I love seeing new sights and meeting new people. What I don't love is packing! It's really hard for me; I always want to bring everything in my closet, but I've learned that it's best to travel light. If you're smart about it, you can pack just a few pieces that you can mix and match into a bunch of different looks. I am proud to say I went to Toronto for two months with just one bag, and I never ran out of clothes. Here are my tips for being a great road warrior!

- **Start with the essentials.** Underwear, bras, socks. Then lay out all the clothes for your entire trip. It's important to know what activities you'll be doing (e.g., sightseeing, surfing, going to a special event) and the local weather forecast. I usually wind up editing out about half of the pieces (don't need it; doesn't go with anything; etc.).

- **You want things you can switch up.** You don't need a new outfit for every single day. So maybe you pack a pair of blue jeans and a pair of colored jeans and then a whole bunch of different tops you can wear with both pants. Choose pieces that can do double duty. For example, a pair of sparkly sandals can be comfy for trekking around during the day and also look glam at night.

- **Pick colors that work well together.** Tempting as it is to toss in your fave neon-yellow skirt, if it doesn't go with anything else, leave home without it!

- **Make sure you include "layering" pieces.**

This includes items such as a hoodie or a sweater that you can pull on or peel off, depending on the temperature.

- **Roll softer clothes.** Tees, tanks, and sweaters can be wrapped like you would wrap a burrito! Then fold larger ones (jackets, dresses, and pants). I also like to pack more delicate stuff like undies in a small bag inside my luggage.

- **Pack heavier items like shoes in a plastic bag.** That way they won't get your clothes dirty. Then put them at the bottom of your bag so they won't crush everything.

- **Pack all makeup and toiletries in a leakproof bag.** Make sure all caps are on tight; the last thing you want is a shampoo explosion!

- **If possible, wear your jacket when you travel,** so you don't have to pack it. Jackets take up a lot of space in a suitcase. I'm always chilly on a plane, so this works for me!

- **Don't overpack or overstuff.** Your clothes will wind up a wrinkled wreck. You can put a few sheets of tissue paper or plastic (like dry cleaning bags) between the layers as well to prevent wrinkles.

- **Finally, leave home anything you can't bear to break or lose.** Why risk it?

STYLE Q&A WITH ZENDAYA:

What should I wear . . .

When it's the first day of school. I say, be cute but casual. I remember when I was really little, like in kindergarten or first grade, I wore a super-fancy dress for the first day. It was kind of itchy and way too princessy for playing in the yard! Now I know that the first day is all about making a good first impression on your teachers and peers. You want to choose an outfit that looks put-together and makes you feel confident. I would also pick a bright color that gives you energy. That first day back after a long summer break can be a tough one!

For class picture day. The cool thing is, you really don't have to worry about your bottom half. Your portrait is shot from the waist up, and in your class pic, you're usually sitting down or standing behind people. Focus on your top. What colors flatter your face? I'd recommend a brighter hue that pops. Also, stay away from any shirt with a big symbol or logo on it—that will distract from your beautiful face!

To a birthday party. If it's not your b'day, you don't want to be too dressed up. Taking attention away from the guest of honor is a no-no! I like a festive shirt with beaded or sequin details paired with colored jeans.

To impress my crush. Be you. Go with something that represents your personal style—and accessorize it with a smile.

To a fancy event. It's a good idea to own one elegant dress for these special occasions. It doesn't have to be a pricey ball gown; just something simple and chic. I love a red A-line dress; you can dress it up or down. I think it's a bit more fun than a little black dress. Pair it with heels and a small clutch, and you're good to go!

BEAUTY ON THE BRAIN ♥

Mix It Up!

You don't have to always wear one color or pattern.
Have fun being a mix master!
Here's how to pull it off like a pro:

❀ **Pair a patterned jacket (stripes, plaid, or animal print) with solid-colored pants** or a skirt that picks up one of the colors in the pattern.

❀ **Space the patterns out.** Pair a thin-stripe blazer with bold leopard-print leggings or a camo cropped sweater with a floral skirt. Wear a bright-colored tee or tank to avoid a potential clash!

❀ **Play with a hint of pattern.** You can choose a print scarf, vest, pair of shoes, bag, or headband that's different from your bottom and not worry about it looking too crazy. It's just a small detail that adds a new layer of interest to your outfit.

❀ **Choose different patterns in the same color family,** like a zebra-print shirt with a black-and-white polka-dot skirt. The color relationship makes the look less chaotic.

❀ **Mix textures.** Right now, I'm loving leather paired with denim. I also think it's cool to mix sheer and heavy fabrics, like leather and lace.

❋ Just Askin':
Fretting over four eyes

I just got glasses, and now I have to go to school looking like a nerd! Everyone is going to tease me and call me "Four-Eyes"!

Hang on! Glasses are pretty cool, in my opinion! Have you seen all those amazing frames and all the hot celebs who are rocking them these days? My friend has these geek glasses that look so funky and edgy on her—I love the shape. When I was in second grade, the doctor told me I needed glasses. I think my parents were worried I would be embarrassed, but I actually thought this was good news. I thought they made me look more mature and smarter and cool. I was actually disappointed when my eyes corrected themselves and I didn't need the glasses anymore! This doesn't happen to a lot of people, so I guess I was lucky. But I do miss my specs!

I get that you're worried (this is not second grade, after all). Specs are a new look for you, and you're not sure how your friends and classmates will respond. But if you walk into that classroom with your head held high, I promise you, things will go better than you think. I say, treat glasses as just another cool accessory! I know some girls who actually collect frames to wear with different outfits. But if they're making you feel that uncomfortable, talk to your parents about when it would be the right time to get contacts.

To Sum It Up:

Style is all about you. If we all dressed alike, the world would be a very boring place! Now is the time to get into your personal fashion groove. Don't let friends or trends dictate how you look. You set the rules . . . and break them!

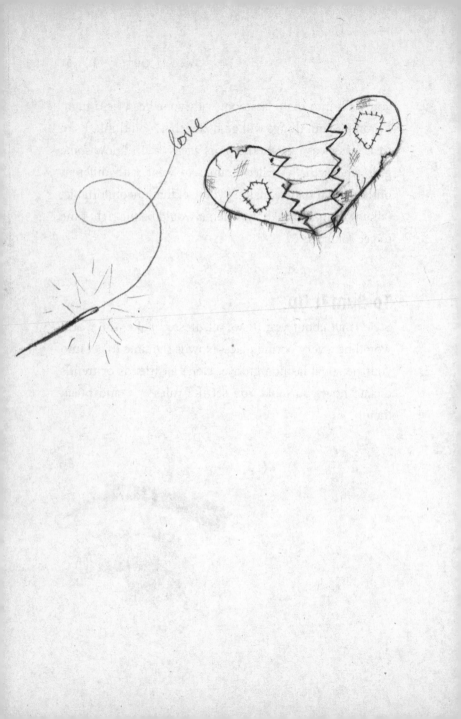

Chapter 4

B'day Parties

When I was in elementary school, I thought a great birthday consisted of a game of musical chairs, a piñata, and a goody bag. Things were so simple back then!

But everything changes when you hit double digits. Tween and teen parties are more about the mood and the moment. Take my fourteenth birthday party. I invited a whole bunch of people for a night of karaoke. Everyone got onstage and made total fools out of themselves in front of the microphone (including me). Best night ever!

If you're considering throwing your first tween b'day

bash, you're in good hands. I am all about the details! For my Sweet Sixteen, I had a "La Dolce Sedicenne," which means "Sweet Sixteen" in Italian. I think it's a fun twist on a traditional b'day bash. I had Italian food, cannolis, and great music. The color scheme was hot pink, electric blue, lime green, and gray. Which brings us to . . .

Setting a Theme

What I like about choosing a theme is that it helps you focus your ideas for your party. If you know your theme is, say, 1950s sock hop, then you can make your play-list (lots of tunes from *Grease*); decide on the decor (old 45 records, photos of Elvis and James Dean); finalize your menu (ice-cream sodas, mini burgers); and suggest costumes for guests (poodle skirts, saddle shoes, leather jackets). See how it all comes together? Think about a hobby, a place, or a decade that you love. Here are a few fun ones:

◆ **Hawaiian luau.** Break out the leis, the limbo stick, and the ukulele! Serve up tropical smoothies (see recipe) with tiny umbrellas and chicken-pineapple skewers! Don't you just "lava" this idea?

DIY: Hawaiian Tropical Smoothies
Makes 12 servings

Serve these up in bright-colored plastic cups with straws and colorful drink umbrellas.

Ingredients:
    6 mangoes (peeled and seeded)
    6 papayas (peeled and seeded)
    3 cups fresh strawberries
    2 cups orange juice
    30 cubes of ice

Ask an adult to help with the dicing and slicing (and generally anything with sharp blades—better safe than sorry!). Place proportional amounts of each ingredient into an electric blender (as much as will fit). Blend until smooth. Pour into glass. Repeat until all ingredients have been used. Then, enjoy!

◆ **Hooray for Hollywood!** Come as your favorite star, from Marilyn or Madonna to the cast of *Twilight*. Roll out a red carpet, hand out "Oscars" for best costumes; serve sparkling apple cider in champagne flutes and star-shaped snacks (see recipe below). Break up into teams for a game of movie trivia, and have everyone "autograph" your fave movie poster as a keepsake.

DIY: Star Snacks
Makes approx. 50 mini stars

Ingredients:
 1 (11 oz.) pkg. refrigerated pizza dough
 Flour
 1 slightly beaten egg white
 1½ tsp. grated Parmesan cheese
 Sliced cheese (your favorite kind will do)
 Star fruit

Unroll pizza dough and sprinkle lightly with flour so it doesn't stick. Use a rolling pin to roll into a 14" x 10" rectangle. Press a small star-shaped cookie cutter into dough to make stars. Transfer stars to ungreased cookie sheet. Brush with egg white and sprinkle with cheese. Bake at 400°F for about eight minutes until lightly golden.

Serve on a platter garnished with slices of cheese (you can cut them into star shapes as well) and star fruit.

◆ **Spa party:** Invite your besties over for a night of pampering! Break out the nail polish for mani/pedis (see below); set out different facial masks (and don't forget the cucumber slices for your eyes!); hand out pretty nail files or flip-flops as party favors. Serve up some "spa cuisine": chilled gazpacho, fruit salad, soothing teas.

DIY: Funky French Mani

Instead of the usual white tip, here's a cool spin.

1. File, soak, and buff nails for a smooth foundation.
2. Choose a bright color for the base. Apply two coats and let dry completely.
3. For the tips, paint a straight line with a metallic or contrasting bright-colored polish (I like the look of pink and red together!). You can also use a quick-dry nail pen. Let dry completely.
4. Finish with top coat to seal.

◆ **Runway show:** Ask each girl to wear an outfit
she'd like to strut like a supermodel! Roll out the
runway (a yard of fabric will do!) and stick it to the
floor with double-sided tape. Offer tiaras, boas, and
sunglasses to accessorize. Crank up the tunes (see
playlist below) and snap lots of pics. You can burn
them on to CDs and hand them out as party favors!
For treats, bake fashion-inspired cookies using
cutters shaped like shoes, hats, and bags. Give your
guests icing and sprinkles to "design" their cookies.

DIY: Tunes for the Runway

Put these on your playlist and crank it up!

"Firework" (Katy Perry)
"Swag It Out" (Guess who? Zendaya!)
"Fashion Is My Kryptonite" (Me and Bella Thorne!)
"Supermodel" (RuPaul)
"Vogue" (Madonna or *Glee* version)

✳ Just Askin':
What about me?

This girl in my sixth-grade class that I thought I was good friends with didn't invite me to her sleepover party. Should I confront her or let it go?

I would let it go—she may have a perfectly good reason for not asking you to come over (maybe her parents would only allow her to invite a certain number of girls, or perhaps she's limiting her guest list to camp pals or cousins). Try not to take it personally. Use this as an opportunity to do something else that makes you happy. Have fun with your friends or family that night.

You're Invited!

Whether you send out e-vites or put them in snail mail, make sure you include:

 Who's throwing the party

 The theme/any required costumes or dress

 The occasion (b'day, holiday, etc.)

 When it starts and ends (date/times)

 Where it's taking place (address, cross streets)

 Whether it's a drop-off or if parents are welcome as well

 An e-mail and phone number to RSVP

 An RSVP deadline date (I suggest at least a week or two before the party date)

The Gift of Giving

You know when your mom told you, "It's the thought that counts" when it comes to presents? I seriously believe that! I always feel bad when someone spends a lot of money on a gift for me. I don't need you to bust open your piggy bank to prove you're my bud! I think the best presents are ones that come from the heart—something sentimental, or even a joke gift that will crack me up. The coolest gift I ever got was from my dad. When I first moved out to L.A., my mom had to stay back home in Oakland to take care of our house before she could join us. I was really missing her. So for my b'day, he surprised me by flying her down here. I was so happy and really touched that my father was so tuned in to my feelings, he knew just what I wanted more than anything in the world.

DIY: Great gifts for your BFF that cost (almost!) nothing

- ✂ A scrapbook filled with pics of you and your BFF over the years

- ✂ A homemade frame with a pic of the two of you

- ✂ A playlist with all your pal's favorite songs

- ✂ A homemade treat she loves (brownies, cookies, cupcakes, etc.)

- ✂ A list of everything you like about your bestie (rolled up and tied with a bow!)

- ✂ A collage of her fave celeb crushes to hang on her wall or in her locker

- ✂ A handmade card with a heartfelt poem ("Roses are red, violets are blue, who's my best friend? That would be you!")

✳ Just Askin':
Dance dilemma

My school is having a formal for the seventh grade, and all my friends are psyched to slow-dance with boys. I have no idea how to dance! What if I step on someone's feet?

You don't have to do anything you don't want to—which includes dance with a guy. But I'd advise you to make the most of it. Have fun! Try not to worry so much about what other people might think, and just enjoy. No one's expecting you to take home the Mirror Ball Trophy from *Dancing with the Stars*! And chances are, your dance partner is feeling just as nervous as you. Maybe you could ask one of the guy friends you're comfortable with, so it won't be so awkward? You can also practice at home first—don't discount your dad for showing you some moves. Mine is pretty smooth!

✳ Just Askin':
Dance dilemma

Everyone saw me wipe out doing a dance move at my friend's birthday party. I am so embarrassed! How can I show my face in school?

Come on, everyone trips up, especially when you're having a ball at a bash and busting some moves. Sometimes when I'm in rehearsal, I zig when I should zag, and my feet get all tangled up . . . and, well, you know where this is going: wipe-out! There I am, on my butt on the floor, and I can feel all eyes on me. So what do I do? I laugh it off! In fact, I call attention to it: "Hey, did you guys just see me do that? I'm such a klutz!" It's better to have people laugh *with* you than *at* you—so remember that for next time. For now, put it behind you. Dancing is fun, and you should never let a kink in your choreography stand in the way!

How Sweet It Is

Okay, let me be perfectly honest here: I am a chocolate lover. So if there's a party with a chocolate fountain, I am so there! Likewise a bash that includes cupcakes, brownies, and devil's food anything. A lot of people feel this way, so when you're planning your birthday, here are some suggestions on how to sweeten the celebration:

A DIY ice-cream sundae bar. Put out all the toppings (syrup, assorted sprinkles, gummy bears, cherries, whipped cream—you name it) and hand each partygoer a bowl with a scoop.

A cupcake tower. This is a really fun alternative to a cake, and it looks pretty impressive piled high on tiers. You can order one or make your own by stacking cupcakes on cardboard boxes covered in pretty paper or fabric.

Fondue fun. Melt some chocolate and have your guests dip in chunks of fruit, pound cake—even marshmallows on skewers. Yummmmm!

Make it mini. Whether it's pies, cupcakes, brownie bites, or cheesecake, you can downsize it and pass it out on platters (see recipe on the next page).

Itty-Bitty No-Bake Cheesecakes
Makes 24

Ingredients:
- 12 vanilla wafer cookies
- 8 oz. (1 package) cream cheese, at room temperature
- ½ cup sugar
- 2 Tbs. sour cream
- 2 tsp. fresh lemon juice
- 12 ripe strawberries, quartered

Place the wafer cookies in a plastic bag, and mash with a mallet or large spoon. Line a mini-muffin pan with paper liners, and spoon the crumbs into the bottom of each cup. Press crumbs down firmly with the back of the spoon. In a mixer, blend together the cream cheese and sugar until smooth. Add sour cream and lemon juice until combined. Spoon the filling into the cups and refrigerate for two to four hours until set. Top with a piece of strawberry or two before serving.

✳ Just Askin':
Sweating over a sleepover

I was invited to my friend's eleventh birthday party . . . and it's a slumber party! I have never slept over at anyone's house before, and I'm really nervous. Should I skip it?

Trust me when I tell you you're not alone in this! A lot of girls have trouble sleeping anywhere besides their own bed, and worry about slumber parties. Sleepovers can be stressful: you're not sure you'll know anybody besides the b'day girl; you're afraid you'll be homesick; you're paranoid that you won't sleep a wink. That said, you could also have a great time and bond with a whole new group of girls! I think it's best to go with an open mind and give it a try. Take something that will comfort and distract you, like an iPod filled with your fave tunes. Then go in there with a positive outlook: "I am going to have a blast!" If you still feel nervous, start small. Sleep over at a close friend's in the neighborhood so you can see what it's like.

I promise you'll be safe and have a good time if you just give yourself the chance!

To Sum It Up:

A party is your chance to be with your friends and classmates in a fun setting, sans stress and schoolwork! Whether you're hosting or attending, remember that it's all about having a good time. Can you say "Par-tay!"?

Chapter 5

Crushes

be·long·ing (bi-lŏng'ĭng; -long'-), n. 1. something that belongs. 2. belongings, things that belong to a person; possessions.
be·lov·ed (bi-lŭv'ĭd; -lŭvd'), adj. dearly loved; dear. —n. person who is loved; darling.

I remember being in first grade and thinking that all boys were stupid and had cooties. Wow, have things changed since then! It's totally normal to notice boys when you're a tween. Crushes—whether it's on a hottie you see on TV or in the movies or a dude who's in your pre-algebra class—are totally normal. This may be the first time you or your friends are thinking of someone as a crush and not a friend who's a boy. Or maybe you're tacking Justin Bieber posters up all over your bedroom walls. These emotions can totally sneak up on you, too. Like, all of a sudden, your neighbor who used to tease you and pull your hair smiles, and you feel butterflies in your stomach.

A crush is really just feelings you have for another person. Maybe you have a lot in common—like, he loves basketball, brownies, and Maroon 5. How cool is that? Or maybe you think he has a really great sense of humor and cracks you up. For whatever reason, you find yourself thinking about him a lot. You may be excited and confused by these emotions—where did they come from? What should I do about them? Sometimes, crushes can you make you giddy: you want to shout to the whole world, "I like him!" Other times, you might be totally tongue-tied. Whenever you see him, you stutter and stumble or forget your own name!

The important thing to remember is that we're still young and have plenty of time to deal with things like dating. I'm sixteen, and I haven't even had a boyfriend yet. I'm more focused on my career, school, and friends, so a "relationship" is not a priority in my life right now.

✳ Just Askin':
He loves me, he loves me not

I have a crush on this boy in my homeroom class, but I'm afraid to tell him. What if he doesn't like me?

It's best to just come right out and say it. The longer you wait, the harder it is, and you're wasting all this time and energy stressing. Don't make it a biggie. Be casual and invite him to hang out: "Hey, would you like to maybe grab a slice after school sometime?" Or ask if he wants to get together and study. The worst thing that could happen is he says no—and then you can move on. In my opinion, that would be his loss!

My so-called best friend blabbed! I told her I like this boy in my school, and she ran up to him and told him! How could she do this to me?

You entrusted her with a deep secret and she let you down. That's not honoring your friendship. Sit her down and talk to her about it. Why did she do it? Did she mean well? Did she think she was helping you by breaking the ice? In the future, make sure to keep your crushes confidential if you don't want your secrets spilled.

Will You Be My Valentine?

Ever since I was in kindergarten, I've been giving out those little valentine cards to friends and family. I think it's sweet and a nice way to acknowledge that you like someone and appreciate him or her. Here are a few fun and creative ways to make someone's Hearts Day extra-happy:

♦ **Spell it out.** Use gummy letters or candy to spell out a short message like "U R COOL" on a piece of cardboard.

♦ **Make a sweet treat.** This recipe on the next page doesn't even need baking!

DIY: Crispy Marshmallow Hearts

Ingredients:
    3 Tbsp. butter or margarine
    1 10-oz. package regular marshmallows (or four
        cups mini marshmallows)
    6 cups crispy rice cereal
    Canned frosting or decorating gel

In a microwave-safe bowl, heat butter and marshmallows on high for 3 minutes, stirring after 2 minutes. Stir until smooth. Add cereal. Stir until well coated.

Using a spatula sprayed with cooking spray, evenly press mixture into 13" x 9" pan, also coated with cooking spray. Cool slightly.

Use heart-shaped cookie cutters coated with cooking spray to cut out treats.

Decorate with frosting and write messages with the gel.

- **Sing it!** Make a CD of your fave tunes. Or, if you're a singer/songwriter, record a song and e-mail it!
- **Create your own crossword or word search** with names of people, places, and things you know the recipient likes. If this gift is for your crush, make sure to include YOUR name in the puzzle!

✳ Just Askin':
My best friend's brother

> I am totally crushing on my BFF's brother—and I don't know what to do about it!

Being friends with him is okay—but anything beyond that, your bestie may not appreciate, and that could cause some major drama in your friendship. Just think about how you would feel inviting a friend over to hang when you know she might secretly be there just to scope out your bro! I say crush on the dude from afar—kind of like I do with Channing Tatum!

To Sum It Up:

Crushes are part of being a tween, so don't stress out if you're suddenly feeling all warm and fuzzy every time a certain boy walks by. Just remember to go at your own pace—don't rush into a romance before you're ready to handle it!

Chapter 6

Get on Your Feet!

When you're busy with homework, school, and extracurriculars, I know it can be hard to figure out how to fit exercise into your schedule. But exercise is a key part of leading a healthy lifestyle and feeling your best! That's why it's important to make it a part of your everyday routine—kind of like brushing your teeth. But I don't want you to think of it as a chore. It's fun to get your body moving and your heart pumping, and there are tons of ways to make that happen. I am super lucky that being on *Shake It Up* means I get to dance up a storm. But even if you don't dance, there are so many fun ways to work up a sweat. Being active has always been important to me—before I ever danced, I was a basketball player! My dad wanted me to be the first woman in the NBA!

Fun Is Good for You!

Did you know these games and activities are a great way to get in your daily exercise?

✳ Playing Ultimate Frisbee

✳ Hula hooping

✳ Ice-skating

✳ Walking your dog

✳ Dancing

✳ Bouncing on a trampoline

✳ Flying a kite

✳ Doing cannonballs into a pool

DIY: Everybody Dance Now!

Crank up the tunes, gather your buds, and try these cool dance moves to work up a sweat!

The Grapevine

The Grapevine is a series of crisscross steps linked together. The key is to get into the groove and make those moves smooth! The faster you go, the better the workout!

1. Make sure you have a large open space to dance in.
2. Begin with hands on hips. Take one large sidestep to the right. Step across and in front of the lead foot. Now take another sidestep, then step behind the lead foot. You can do this move once or twice before switching to the other foot.
3. Now repeat to the left side. When you get comfortable with the choreography, increase your speed and move your arms. Personally, I like to fist-pump it!

The Freeze

Imagine paparazzi snapping your picture as you do this

move! You will simply freeze mid-motion as you move your upper body in a box formation. Tighten your stomach muscles as you hit each corner of your (imaginary) box—it's great core work (meaning it tones and tightens your abs and middle section)!

1. Spread your feet shoulder-length apart. Bend forward to the left side of your body using only your upper half. That's the first corner of the box.

2. Now, still bending forward, move to the right. That's the second corner.

3. Still leaning right, raise your torso so that you're standing up. That's the third corner.

4. Now, lean to the left side (your fourth corner) to complete the move. Make sure to keep your feet in place on the ground as you move to the beat. You can move your arms, snap, clap—whatever feels good! If you want to think outside the box—try the same motion in a circle! Just follow the beat and repeat three to five times.

The Step-Out

This funky move with hip-hop roots really gets your heart pumping!

1. Start with feet shoulder-length apart and arms at your sides.
2. Step your right foot in front and to the right, leaning back as you step out. Swing one arm forward and the other back.
3. Step your foot back to the start position. Repeat three to four times.
4. Now step out with the same foot, bending at the waist and leaning forward.
5. Work your arms back and forth as you step out.
6. Switch feet and repeat on the opposite side. You can even alternate leaning forward, then back.
7. Once you master the moves, try doing it faster, to the beat of the music.

How Not to Be a Dance-Floor Dud

The best way to get comfortable on the dance floor is to—you guessed it!—dance! Start in front of your mirror at home, where you don't feel self-conscious. Put on your favorite music, close your eyes, and let your body just move with the rhythm. It's easier than you think. If you want to look even slicker, I recommend doing a little research: watch dance movies or music videos (and of course, *Shake It Up!*) for inspiration. You can even take a dance class to build your confidence and help you master some moves. Remember, it's not a competition; you're just supposed to have fun and cut loose.

*Just Askin':
Don't sweat the small stuff

I sweat a lot in school! What should I do?

Puberty definitely makes you perspire more—and that can lead to body odor (yuck! The dreaded "B.O."). So my advice is to make sure you have a good deodorant. They come in lots of pretty fragrances, or fragrance-free if you have sensitive skin. You can also find different formulas, like roll-on, powder, spray, and clear. Experiment with a few options until you find the right one. Apply in the morning and again after gym or recess to be extra-covered. Once you find the right deodorant for you, you'll be smellin' like a rose!

My feet stink in my high-tops! How do I freshen them?

You don't have to stand for stinky sneakers! There are tons of deodorizing sprays, inserts, even fun little deodorizing balls you can use to freshen up that footwear. I sometimes sprinkle mine with baby powder to absorb moisture. Your best bet is to never go barefoot; socks will absorb sweat and keep your feet from smelling foul.

Eat Your Veggies!

I am lucky that I actually like salad, carrots, and most greens—probably because I'm a vegetarian. I made that decision when I was eleven years old. My fave lunch is a spinach salad with raspberry vinaigrette, dried cranberries, and candied walnuts. Or veggie burritos—yum! So yes, I eat pretty healthy—just not all the time. I can't resist coffee ice cream, and I am completely addicted to cupcakes, chocolate, and just about anything sweet or creamy. But I do try to eat these things in moderation and balance it out with plenty of healthy stuff.

✳ Just Askin':
Weight a second!

The girls in my gym class are always making fun of me. I'm not as skinny as they are. The other day in the locker room, they called me "Blubber Butt"! What should I do?

People come in all shapes and sizes, and those girls shouldn't dictate how you look or criticize you because

First time we met
Davis at his audition,
and I just knew he
had the part!

Like sister,
like brother

Love this girl!

B'day kiss for my little bro!

On set . . . funny faces!

Pilot pickup celebration dinner . . . we were soooo little!

Love these ladies . . . I call fourth McClain sister!! LOL and Adam claims fifth.

Me and my Rody!!
That's Ro and
Brody . . . came up
with it myself!

I love these two . . .
they literally ALWAYS
keep me laughing!

In NYC . . .
gooooood times!

Cast partaaaayyy!!!

Swagged out

Me and my two little
munchkins . . . dawwww!

Mini car photo shoot! LOL

I have a nail obsession!

Me and Dej . . . twinning!

Sweet Sixteen = Pretty in Pink!

The obsession is real!

My amazing stylist LAW . . .
doing his magic, yet again!

"Swag It Out"
video in
Oak-Town!

Z-SWAGG

Me, Deja, and Dominique.
Love these girls!

On our way to Paris!

Music = Life

At the White House . . .
what an amazing experience!

Mikey, Ezenia, Roshon,
and me in NYC.

CAAAAKE!

Beautiful fans in Dubai . . .
can't wait to go back!

Performing back home,
like I never left!

of it. Be comfortable with your body; that's all that matters. Stand up for yourself by setting the record straight and telling those girls in P.E., "That really hurts my feelings, and if I were to say something like that to you, you wouldn't like it. So please don't say it about me or anyone else." If you're afraid to speak up, another great option is to go to an adult you can trust, like your parent or a teacher, and explain that you are being bullied. This is not acceptable and shouldn't happen to you or anyone else.

My best friend is bigger than most girls in our sixth-grade class, and kids have been teasing her and calling her names. I feel bad, but I also don't want people to turn against me! What should I do?

What's more important to you: your friendship or fitting in with a bunch of bullies? Sometimes those girls are the ones with the insecurity issues—so maybe that's why they're picking on your friend. If your bestie is being hurt or bullied by unkind classmates, then you owe it to her to help! Standing by and letting it happen is just as bad as bullying itself. That said, you shouldn't try to take on the meanies single-handedly. Instead, help your friend walk away with her head held high, and assure her that you are there for her. Encourage her to talk to a teacher or her parents and put an end to this. Don't keep bullying a secret—someone else's or yours.

DIY: Five Fab Ways to Motivate a Friend

Everyone gets bummed out now and then. That's what friends are for: to lift you up and inspire you to get back in the game! If you know someone who needs a little bit of cheering:

- **Leave them a silly voice mail message**—like a knock-knock joke or a celeb impression. It'll crack you both up!
- **Put a sticky note in her locker** reminding her "U R AWESOME!"
- **Make a playlist of uplifting tunes.** A personal fave: "Single Ladies" by Beyoncé. It makes me feel invincible!
- **Write her a fan letter!** Include all the things you think are great/special about her.
- **Give her a hug!** Never underestimate the power of a hug from a pal to pick you up when you're feeling down.

DIY: Grandma's Zucchini and Tomato Gratin

My Grandma Daphne lives in Danville, California, and when I lived nearby in Oakland, she used to cook for me a lot. When I was little, I would sleep over at her house one day a week to give my mom a break from me! She would always cook for me and introduce me to new healthy things, which we often cooked together. One of my favorite recipes is below—it's like a pizza, but without the crust! Super-healthy for you—and super-delicious!

Ingredients:
  1½ pounds medium tomatoes, cut into ¼-inch slices
  2 medium zucchini cut in ⅛-inch diagonals
  1 Tbsp. olive oil
  4 garlic cloves, minced
  2 Tbsp. of your favorite dark olives, sliced and pitted (of course!). Grandma uses Kalamata, but black olives from the can work well, too!
  Basil leaves, thinly sliced
  ¾ cup grated Parmesan cheese

Continued on next page.

pinch of salt
pepper to taste

Place tomato slices on a paper towel to pull the water out. Sprinkle with salt. Do the same for the zucchini. Heat the oven to 375°F. With an adult's supervision, heat the oil in a skillet over medium-high heat. Sauté (that's a fancy way to say "cook in the oil!") the zucchini for four minutes, or until golden. Don't crowd the pan or the zucchini will steam, and you want nice caramelization and flavor. Transfer to a plate and let cool.

Layer half of the zucchini slices in a greased 1-quart baking pan. Top with half of the tomatoes. Sprinkle with half the garlic, olives, basil, Parmesan cheese, salt, and pepper. Season with pepper. Repeat again for the second layer using the remaining ingredients. Drizzle a little olive oil over it. Cover with foil and bake for ten minutes. Remove foil and bake for twenty minutes more, or until cheese is melted. Yummy!

You and Your Body

Hey, you say, what is going on with my body? When did I get hair . . . there?! Why don't my clothes fit right? When did I grow a full shoe size? Now's the time when you're going through some weird changes, morphing from girl into woman (and sometimes getting stuck in between!). It's important to remind yourself that we're all not on the same schedule: some girls grow curves much sooner than others. And no two people are exactly alike. Everybody— and every body—is different.

When I was in middle school, I looked in the mirror and saw this tall, skinny girl looking back at me. Hot? Not! But my parents always assured me I was beautiful inside and out—and that helped. Sure, there may be girls (even your besties) who you may think are prettier than you at this stage of the game—and occasionally, you may find yourself wondering, "What's up with that? Why couldn't that be me?" It's okay to feel a little envious of what you don't have. We all do it. But don't let it destroy your confidence.

When you look in the mirror, try not to focus on the flaws (or what you think are flaws!). Instead, take a good, hard look at everything that makes you *you*: your warm brown eyes, your cute freckles, your totally "in" braces.

Then move beyond the physical: ask yourself what qualities make you an awesome friend, a great daughter or sibling, a cool classmate. Focus on the person on the inside till the outside catches up! And it will, I promise!

To Sum It Up:

Happy starts with healthy . . . so take care of yourself! Exercise, eat well, and appreciate all the special qualities that make you YOU!

keep it...

Chapter 7

Mirror, Mirror

Before we shoot an episode of *Shake It Up,* I have to spend a lot of time—sometimes as much as two hours—in the hair and makeup chair. Foundation, mascara, blush, lip gloss—my stylist has to layer it all on me! Sometimes an episode will call for me to glitz it up (lots of sparkly eye shadow for some of those *Shake It Up, Chicago!* numbers); other times, like on the episode "Made in Japan," I had to wear dramatic brows and bright pink lipstick! Even if I'm just playing Rocky at her most casual, the lights and the cameras really make me look pale and pasty, so makeup is a necessity. I'm pretty happy when I take all that makeup off and just let my skin breathe.

But there was a time—not so long ago—when all I wanted to do was wear eyeliner. All my friends in middle school did, but my parents said no. No matter how much I pleaded, they wouldn't let me out of the house with it on. It was not up for discussion, and I thought it was unfair.

Maybe your folks feel the same way. Not every girl in middle school is allowed to wear makeup, and some girls don't even want to. Now that I am older and my parents are cool with it, I understand where they were coming from. They weren't just being difficult; they thought I was naturally beautiful, and I shouldn't hide it. They were trying to teach me that beauty comes from the inside.

That's my advice to you as well—truly, I don't think any girl needs to hide behind a makeup mask. Sure, you'll look older. Anyone who piles on lipstick, shadow, and liner is bound to look more "grown-up" (or like a clown, if you overdo it!). But you also won't look like you. Nowadays, I like to think of makeup as a way to "dress up" my face when I'm going out to a party or a special occasion. If you see me around my home or my dressing room, I'm makeup-free and lovin' the real me!

If you are allowed to wear makeup, and you choose to, then go easy. A tiny bit of foundation, a sweep of blush, and a hint of lip gloss is probably plenty for everyday. For lips, I think a nude peachy gloss with a little shimmer looks good on everyone. You can also slick on some flavored lip balm if you prefer—it will make your smile soft and shiny!

DIY: A Natural Blush

I've watched a lot of YouTube how-tos—and makeup artists in action—to teach myself this technique. This is how the pros advise you do it so you look rosy-cheeked and ready for your special event!

1. Start with the right shade. You want the blush color to closely match the color of your face when it flushes. Gently pinch your cheek, then hold the blush up to compare colors.

2. Consider the formula. Most tween and teen girls have combination skin (both oily and dry)—so a powder blush is probably your best bet. For dry skin, a cream blush is great, and a liquid or gel works well if your face is oily.

3. Use a full-size makeup brush—not the itty-bitty

ones that come with most blush. You want to be able to sweep and blend, not just dot the color on. Stroke the brush across the blush in its container, then tap off any extra powder (this prevents streaking).

4. Now comes my favorite part! Look in the mirror and SMILE BIG. See where the apples of your cheeks are? That's where the blush belongs! After you've brushed on the color, gently blend with a makeup sponge. If the color is a little too intense, you can always wash it off and start again.

Clean Complexion

The most important thing you can do for your skin when you are a tween is take care of it! Follow these tips for a close-up–ready face!

♦ **Go gentle.** Like I said, young skin can be super-sensitive, so you don't want to borrow your mother's cleanser and toner—or even your big sister's. Some girls think that the stronger the cleanser, the better. For tweens, this isn't the case. Stick to a cleanser for sensitive skin—they're gentler

and less likely to cause irritation (a.k.a. breakouts).
Ask your doctor to recommend one if you don't
know which brand to choose.

◆ **Wash up.** Never—I repeat, never!—go to bed
with makeup on! It's the easiest way to clog your
pores and cause a blemish blitz. Wash your skin
every morning before you start the day and every
night before you go to bed with your cleanser
and warm water (not hot!). If you do sports or
dance, it's a good idea to wash your face after
exercising.

◆ **Slather on sun shield.** Sunscreen is so
important! It takes years for damage to show, but
if you go out in the sun unprotected, trust me—
your skin is taking a beating. If you play sports
outdoors or love to bike, hike, or hang at the
beach, make sure you use an SPF of 15 or higher,
and apply it frequently, especially if you sweat
or get wet. Make sure you use a sunscreen that's
specially formulated for the face; some products
can clog pores.

◆ **Keep hair back.** Bangs and long hair can cause
breakouts. If you're playing sports or otherwise
sweating, make sure to tie it back in a pony or a
headband to keep it off your skin.

Face Facts: The Truth About Zits

I am a teen girl, so of course, I have experienced embarrassing pimples. They have a knack for popping up just
when I have something important to do—like an interview or a photo shoot. Most tweens get acne—it comes
with the changes your body goes through during puberty.
The obvious place you get it is on your face, but you can
also get bumps on your neck, back, shoulders, and chest.
There's a big scientific theory for why this happens: basically, the pores in your skin contain oil glands that can
become overactive when you're a tween and teen. Pores
get clogged; bacteria gets trapped inside, and you've got
the start of acne. It isn't pretty, but it's so common! Eighty
percent of kids will deal with it—so if you are experienc-
ing an acne outbreak, you're in good company. The best
way to battle blemishes is to know what causes them and
how to heal and prevent them.

A POP QUIZ ON PIMPLES!

Answer true or false to the following and check your answers on the next page:

1. T If I have a zit on my face I should NEVER squeeze it.

2. F Eating chocolate causes pimples.

3. F Sitting in the sun heals acne.

4. F To prevent pimples, I should scrub my face with a washcloth.

5. T I should look for products that are labeled "noncomedogenic."

ANSWERS

1. TRUE: Playing with a pimple (poking, squeezing, touching it in general) can make it worse. You could actually be infecting it with the oil from your hands and causing permanent scars. Treat it with an over-the-counter acne cream, or talk to your doctor about other options.

2. FALSE: This is a big myth! But some people may have certain food sensitivities and allergies that can make acne worse. Talk to your doctor if you notice that your skin flares up when you eat specific things.

3. FALSE: A tan may help camouflage acne temporarily, but sitting in the sun (and sweating!) can produce more oil on your face, which can actually make your pimples worse.

4. FALSE: This may actually irritate your skin and pores more! Wash your face gently with a simple daily facial cleaner, and dot on some spot treatment every now and then.

5. TRUE: If you wear sunscreen or makeup, look for this word on the label. It means the ingredients in the product won't clog pores.

✳ Just Askin':
Cover up

> I have a really bad zit on my
> forehead—how can I hide it?

Sometimes, no matter what you do, a pimple pops up
when you least expect it—and least want it! No biggie.
My makeup artist showed me a quick cover-up routine
that makes a zit virtually invisible. Start with a clean face.
If you use acne spot treatment, dab some on and let it
dry. Now choose a concealer that's the same color as the
skin on your face (not lighter; this will draw attention to
the zit!). Dab it on with a clean cotton swab or a sponge,
not your fingers (they contain oil that can aggravate it).
Using a sponge, apply a dot of foundation, also in your
skin tone, to the area. Blend well and set with a dusting
of loose translucent powder. Now where did that nasty
zit go?

I have "back-ne!" I'm so embarrassed—
especially when I have to change in
the locker room! Why did this happen?

This is a very common problem for tweens and teens—
and even adults. Pimples don't always pop up on your
face. Sometimes they can appear your body as well—in
many cases, on the back and chest. Experts say to make
sure your clothes are not the culprit—like, make sure
your tennis team uniform isn't too tight (and causing fric-
tion) up top. Sweat can also aggravate acne, so shower as
soon as possible after exercising. You can even ask your
doctor if there is a special cleanser you can use to prevent
and heal acne.

Posing for Picture Day

I don't know about you, but class pictures were never my
fave head shots. I would always forget when Picture Day
was, so I'd come unprepared! I would be in some horrible
outfit with my hair all crazy, and I'd run to the bathroom,
put some water in my curls, and try to make miracles

happen! The pics were never that horrible . . . but it was always a close call! So my advice is be prepared. There are a few things you can do to ensure you look your best:

- **Practice your smile in the mirror.** I know it sounds a little silly, but this will help you get a feel for how to grin in front of the camera. Teeth or no teeth? Small or wide? See what looks best. Also, look at yourself from different angles. Everyone has a better side—what's yours?

- **Don't try anything new the day before.** By this I mean a new hairstyle, a new brand of makeup, or face lotion. The last thing you want is for your skin to freak or your hair to look crazy— and you can't fix it in twenty-four hours!

- **Choose your outfit carefully.** A lot of kids go for dark tops (like navy blue, black, or brown) since it makes your face stand out. I think the prettiest picture outfits are bright and cheerful and give your face a warm glow.

- **Keep accessories simple.** No jumbo earrings or multiple strands of necklaces. You don't want your bling to take attention away from your beautiful face!

- **Sit up straight.** No slouching (like your mom always tells you!). Shoulders back, head high. Look

straight into the camera and try to make your eyes
twinkle with energy and excitement!

♦ **Pack supplies.** Put a small brush/comb, lip gloss,
pocket mirror, etc. in your schoolbag for a quick
touch-up before you say "Cheese!"

DIY: Let's Have a Spa-liday!

As I mentioned in Chapter Four, spa-themed parties are
a lot of fun. This is one of my fave things to do with my
friends! We create an at-home spa and take turns getting
pampered. It's super-fun and relaxing, and you can find
most of the ingredients right in your own kitchen. Make
sure you ask a parent for permission or help if you're
going to be making "recipes" in the kitchen. Also, test
each recipe on a small patch of skin on your arm before
applying to your face.

✳ ✸ ✳ ✸ ✳ ✸ ✳ ✸ ✳ ✸ ✳ ✸ ✳

Tutti-Fruity Facial
You'll need:
½ cup chilled and crushed pineapple
½ cup chilled mango slices

½ cup chilled green tea

¼ cup honey

Place fruit in blender and puree. Pour into a bowl and add tea and honey. Mix well. Apply to your face (be careful not to get it in your eyes!). Let set for twenty minutes, then rinse off with warm water.

• • • • • • • • • • • • • • • •

Berry Beautiful Mask

You'll need:

1 cup strawberries

Juice of 1 lemon

½ cup plain yogurt

Place the berries in a blender. Add the lemon juice and yogurt and mix well. Refrigerate mixture for thirty minutes, then apply to face, being careful to avoid the eyes. Leave on for thirty minutes, then wash off with cool water. Refreshing!

• • • • • • • • • • • • • • • •

Papaya Hair Smoothie

You'll need:

½ ripe papaya (remove skin and seeds)

½ cup plain yogurt

Place papaya in blender and blend until smooth. Add yogurt. Apply mixture to ends of hair and let sit for thirty minutes to repair split ends. For extra conditioning, wrap hair in plastic wrap or a warm towel after applying smoothie. Wash hair as usual and rinse well.

• •

Avocado Moisturizer

You'll need:

1 ripe avocado (remove pit and skin)

¼ cup olive oil

In a large bowl, mash avocado. Drizzle in olive oil till you get a creamy consistency. Apply to hands and/or feet and cover with plastic wrap. Let sit for twenty minutes. Rinse with warm water for silky-smooth hands and feet!

✳ ❀ ✳ ❀ ✳ ❀ ✳ ❀ ✳ ❀ ✳ ❀ ✳

✳ Just Askin':
Model envy

> Every time I look at a magazine cover and see a celeb, I am totally jealous. They look so amazing! Why can't I look like that?

Why? Because no one looks like that! Take it from someone who has been in magazines—and knows what goes into making someone look good on a cover. First of all, there's hair and makeup—sometimes as much as several hours of primping! Then there's retouching, a magic-eraser computer program that wipes away everything from wrinkles and dark circles to blemishes and cellulite. After all that, of course the girl on the cover looks gorgeous!

We're literally being bombarded by images in magazines, movies, and on TV with a standard of beauty that's impossible to achieve. So don't buy into it. Instead, focus on what your mind and spirit do—not how your body looks at this moment (because it's changing every day!). My parents always remind me that we have our bodies not so we can compare them to others but so they can help us rock the world!

DIY: A Perfect Pedi

Give your toes a little TLC with an at-home pedicure:

1. **Remove all old polish** and clip your nails straight across (you may want to ask your mom for help). Then soak your feet in a basin (or bathtub) filled with warm, soapy water.

2. **Massage your feet with a good moisturizer.** Use a cotton ball dipped in nail polish remover to clean lotion off the nails for a fresh surface.

3. **Roll the polish bottle between your palms** to mix the color. Don't shake; this can cause bubbles in the polish.

4. **Apply a base coat.** Let dry three minutes.

5. **Apply first coat of color.** Let dry five minutes.

6. **Apply second coat.** Let dry five minutes.

7. **Apply top coat.** Then use a cotton swab dipped in nail polish remover to clean up any smudges around the edges of the nails.

8. **Let dry for at least thirty minutes.** I like to use the time to kick up my feet, chillax, and listen to some tunes or call a friend!

New Nail Looks

Nail polish doesn't have to be plain! There are so many cool new ones to choose from. I like to do nail art designs on my hands every week, everything from Michael Jackson's "Thriller"-themed nails to black with white tips. I usually go to a salon and let the pros work their magic—but you can also get creative at home. Check out your local drugstore or makeup store for these fun finger trends.

Matte: Instead of shiny, these colors are intensely dramatic! When you paint them on, they look like velvet.

Sequins: These polishes come with built-in glitz. So glam for a special occasion!

Holographic hues: Polishes that have a 3-D shimmer!

Mood polish: Changes color in the light or when your hands get warm or cold.

Nail pens: Use nail pens to draw on cool pics and shapes—a different one on each digit, if you choose.

✳ Just Askin':
Nail nibbler

Help!
I can't stop biting my nails!
I know it's a bad habit!

Have no fear—this is one bad habit you can break. My sister used to bite her nails, and we put this gross-tasting stuff on them (they sell it in drugstores). Every time she'd taste it, she'd make a face and stop. The bigger question is, why are you biting your nails? Are you stressed out or nervous? If so, try to find another outlet, like squeezing a stress ball, going for a run, shooting some hoops—anything that will get your anxiety out and save your poor digits from attack! I also think getting a mani can really help. You'll be less tempted to sabotage your nails if they're pretty and coated in polish!

I want to wear neon nail polish, but my ballet teacher won't let us! I'm so bummed!

Don't be bummed! There are so many cool temporary ways to dress up your nails! There are lots of stick-on and paint-and-peel options, so you can polish your nails for a special occasion and not make your teacher see red. They come in all kinds of cool colors and patterns—even metallic! I also think it's pretty to wear clear polish or buff your nails to a natural shine, so don't rule those options out, either.

To Sum It Up:

Your skin may do some pretty crazy things as you inch your way toward being a grown-up. It happens to all of us, so don't think you're the only one with zits or stinky pits. A few extra steps in your routine will make it totally manageable. For special occasions, have fun with makeup and nails. I think of my fancy fingers as an accessory!

Chapter 8

Brush Up

We all want what we don't have, right?

In my case, it was straight hair. I have naturally curly brown hair, and I was always envious of girls in elementary school who had long, stick-straight, shiny hair. I whined to my mom, "It's just so unfair!" They looked like princesses; I looked like a poodle! Or at least, that's what I thought when I was younger. Around fifth grade, I decided to embrace what I was born with and just let my hair wave as much as it wanted. Wow—it was pretty awesome. I loved it! The moral of my "hair-story": work with what you got, and you'll look (and feel!) gorgeous.

DIY: Quick Curls

If you don't have a ton of time to play with styling tools, these easy tricks will help you have a head of gorgeous waves!

◆ **Wash your hair before you go to bed at night.** Roll small sections (one to two inches) of your hair in sponge curlers and sleep in them (they're soft and won't bother you). When you get up in the morning, just take the curlers out, run your fingers through your hair, add some hair spray, and go.

◆ **Braid your hair in one, two, or several mini braids** when it's wet. In the morning, take out the braid(s), and you'll have cool crimps!

◆ **If you shower in the morning, apply mousse to slightly damp hair and scrunch.** Allow your hair to air-dry for a tousled look.

◆ **When hair is damp, put it up in a loose bun.** The longer you leave it in, the more volume and wave your hair will have.

✳ Just Askin':
Hair help

The nurse sent me home from school today with lice! Now everyone is going to make fun of me—or stay far away! Ew, I feel gross!

This is a very common problem among kids! It's icky (and itchy!), but not the end of the world. Don't freak; your parents and pediatrician can help you get rid of it with an over-the-counter kit or other treatment. You may also have to take special steps to clean your house and your clothes. But you'd be surprised at how many kids in your class have had it and will understand. If people say something to you, then just ignore it—or assure them that it's all under control. Lice have nothing to do with being dirty—so don't feel gross! In fact, lice prefer clean, healthy heads. Once you lose the lice, prevention is key. Remember not to share hats, brushes, combs, barrettes, headbands, etc.

I got the worst haircut! The stylist completely chopped my bangs, and now I look ridiculous!

The good news is, hair grows back—so your bangs are only a temporary situation. In the meantime, get creative! Think of this as a styling challenge. Hold your bangs back with a cute barrette or braid, or twist them out of your face and secure with a sparkly clip. A little hair gel will help slick them to the side, and a headband can smooth them away. Next time, make sure you and your stylist are on the same page. If he/she doesn't hear ya . . . time to switch salons!

Getting the Style You Want

Every girl has a hair horror story—a stylist who cut off too much ("If I wanted to look like my little brother, I would have said so!"), or a do that was so completely not you that it brought you to tears. Been there. The key is communication. You have to make sure you that you're being clear with your stylist about what you like and don't like. She's a hairdresser, not a psychic! Speak up!

Be reasonable. Are you asking for a curly style when you have stick-straight hair? As fab as your stylist may be, he or she isn't a miracle worker. Ask for something beyond your hair's limitations, and you're not going to be happy with it.

Show as well as tell. Flip through celeb and hair magazines and tear out pics of the styles you like. Then you can hand it to the stylist and say, "I want this look." Or you can mix it up: choose the length from one style, the side-swept bangs from another. Make sure you ask what's involved in the upkeep: will you be able to achieve this style yourself when not in the salon chair? Is J.Lo's new do really something you want for middle school?

Don't just say "trim it." To one stylist, that can mean cutting off an inch. To another . . . a buzz cut! Show the length of hair that you'd like trimmed with your fingers when hair is DRY, or specify a measurement: "Take off a half inch only." Be sure to trim hair every couple of months so it stays healthy.

Share with your stylist what a day in your life is like. Are you super-busy? Do you need a more simple wash-and-go style? Or are you a social butterfly and want a super-versatile style that goes from casual to dressy easily?

Fess up about your hair's problems. Does it fall flat? Frizz up? This can help the stylist decide on the cut. Plus, you'll get advice on products and care.

DIY: Five 5-Minute Dos

I love to wear my hair in all different ways: up, down, back, forward, curly, straight. You name it, I've tried it. That's the fun of being a girl! I've even played with temporary looks using clip-in feathers, extensions, and hair wraps (got an awesome one with beads recently!). But these are definitely my fave styles that I think look great on practically everyone (mid to long hair, any texture works best). An added bonus: they take just five minutes!

Note: Before you get started on any of these styles, make sure your hair has been brushed through and is tangle-free!

The Almost-Updo
I love this for parties—any occasion that's just a little fancy!

1. Use your index fingers to pull hair straight back from behind your ears,

and separate this section from the rest of
your hair.

2. With a clip or hair tie, secure the section
of hair you've separated into a pony. The
rest of your hair should fall free.

3. You can pull a few tendrils loose at the
sides or side-sweep a bang.

The Fancy Pony

A little more polished than a sporty pony; I would wear
this look to school.

1. Using an elastic, make a high or low
pony (your choice), but leave a one-
inch-wide strand loose underneath the
gathered hair.

2. Wrap the one-inch section around the
base of the ponytail several times, completely covering the elastic.

3. Use a hairpin to secure the end of the
wrapped strand to the base of the ponytail, or tuck the strand under the elastic.

The Messy Bun

On hectic mornings when I'm running late, this look
gives me instant style!

1. Brush hair into a ponytail. Use one hand to hold the pony base, the other to twist the pony up into a loose coil. This is the bun.
2. Use bobby pins to secure the bun, leaving a few ends sticking out to give it a "carefree" look.
3. Spritz lightly with hair spray to hold in place.

Triple Twist

Flirty and fun, this is one do you can do in a flash!

1. Part hair in the middle.
2. Create three small twisted sections: one at the part and one at each temple.
3. Pull the twists back, gather at the crown, and connect with bobby pins.
4. Spritz lightly with hair spray to hold in place.

Loose Side Braid

Braids may be for little kids, but this carefree version is way more mature.

1. Using a brush, gather hair to one side so it almost covers one ear.

2. Divide hair into three sections and braid loosely. Tie it off at the bottom with an elastic.

3. Allow the braid to drape in front of one shoulder (this style works best with long hair).

4. Add a headband for a "tiara" effect. So pretty!

✳ Just Askin':
Tangle tricks

My older sister told me my hair looks like a bird's nest. It's long, and it's always getting tangled and matted, especially in the morning. Any ideas?

I know from experience that curly and wavy hair can get very knotty. If the a.m. is your biggest issue, then make sure you prep your hair at night. Spray on a detangler/leave-in conditioner after you shower, and run through it with a "wet brush" specially made for detangling or with a wide-tooth comb. Then put your hair into one or two loose braids before you go to bed. When you wake up, you'll have soft waves and no knots!

I blew a bubble and got gum stuck in my hair! Now what?

This sticky situation is easy to solve . . . with peanut butter! Experts say to rub some creamy peanut butter into the gummy spot. Because it's sticky, it stays in place while the oil eats away at the gum (baby oil, cooking spray, and olive oil will also do the trick). Then wash it out with soap and water, and you're good to go. Next time, watch where you're popping!

To Sum It Up:
Your hair is your crowning glory! Whatever locks you were born with, love them and take good care of them. And whenever you have the chance to try out a new style, go for it. Have fun and show off your hair flair.

Chapter 9

Meet the Parents

When you were younger, your parents controlled everything: what you wore, where you went, the people you hung out with, even what time you went to bed. But now that you're a tween, you probably feel like you want to start having more of a say. That's cool . . . but moms and dads don't always appreciate that you want to make your own decisions. They may see your declaration of independence as a diss.

I hear from a lot of kids who feel that their parents are unfair and don't understand them. But here's the thing: no matter how much you disagree with them, no matter how much they embarrass you (my mom used to call me "Poopie" in public!), your parents mean well and have your back. They're not trying to cramp your style or spoil your fun. They love you and want you to be the very best person you can be.

I'm lucky to have a very open and honest relationship with my mom and dad. I think they trust me because I tell them everything. But that isn't to say they don't set some pretty tight rules. They expect me to do well in school—when I got a bad grade on a spelling test because I didn't study . . . well, it wasn't pretty! They made me spend the whole weekend (well, not the *whole* weekend . . . but you know what I mean!) writing the words I got wrong over and over! They've also been pretty strict when it comes to boys: no dating till I turned sixteen! And when I first got my Facebook account, my mom checked it constantly to see what I was writing (and posted comments on my updates—how embarrassing!).

I've never been seriously grounded, but I have gotten my computer and phone privileges restricted when I didn't clean up my room or got a little "cheeky!" But as I have grown up, my parents have given me more freedom and privacy because I have proved to them that I am worthy of their trust and respect. Of course, there are days I kinda wish I could just crawl into my mom's lap for a hug!

Maybe you're in that place now. You're feeling this emotional tug-of-war between wanting to be grown-up and wanting to stay a kid. Your parents are also probably freaked out about it—it's hard to see their baby growing up so fast! So cut them some slack. Be patient; be respectful. Try to understand where they're coming from when they say and do things you may not agree with.

Also keep in mind that every family is different and has a different set of rules. Just because your BFF's mom lets her stay up till eleven on school nights doesn't mean that your parents will let you do the same. My dad loves to say, "If everyone is standing on their head, does that mean that you should, too?" Translation: He doesn't buy the old "everyone is doing it!" excuse. I used to think that was unfair . . . now I actually see how smart it is. My parents have always wanted me to be strong and dance to my own beat, and that's how they've raised me.

✳Just Askin':
Family feuds

> I got a D on my math test, so my mom
> grounded me—no TV, computer, or cell
> phone for a month! What can I do to get
> her to give me a break?

I know this is really hard to do (I'm not sure I could actually survive very long without my cell phone!), but go with what she says. I know it's going to be rough, but you did the crime . . . so now do the time. If you want to reduce your sentence, then show her how mature and responsible you can be. Study like crazy for the next test. Clean your room and wash the dishes. Actions speak louder than words. And if you really are struggling in math, then be honest about it. Tell your mom you need help from a teacher or a tutor. Once she sees that you're actually taking action to improve your grades, she'll start giving your stuff back. Remember, it's only temporary! You're not going to be grounded for life!

I told my mom I was going to the library . . . but I was really hanging out at the mall with my friends. She found out and was furious that I lied to her. Now she won't let me leave the house except to go to school!

Honesty is the best policy. You have so much more freedom when your parents trust you, and you have to earn that trust. By grounding you, your mom is trying to make a point: she expects you to tell her the truth. If you don't, you're going to be on lockdown. Otherwise, how can your mom be sure you are safe? What if there was an emergency and she needed you? What if there was a serious situation at the library and she was concerned for your safety? Or if something happened at the mall, and she didn't know you were there? Your mom doesn't want to stalk you; she just wants to protect you. So my advice is to ride this out, and the next time you want to hang with your friends, ask her permission. If she says no, then tell her you'll respect her wishes but you'd like her to consider letting you go next time. Eventually, you'll earn her respect . . . and a "go to the mall" pass!

I'm always fighting with my parents over everything! Is there any way we can get along better?

There's a lot you can do! First off, pick your battles wisely. Fighting doesn't always solve things. Is it worth starting World War III to get your way . . . or is it possible that your parents have a good point? Try not to blow your top every time you and your parents disagree. Instead, take a deep breath, count to ten, and give yourself a "time-out." Consider what you would do if you and your BFF had a disagreement. Would you scream and slam the door in her face? I doubt it. You'd try to keep your cool and communicate. Try to remember this when you and your folks don't see eye-to-eye. Remind yourself that everyone is entitled to an opinion. That goes for both you and your parents. It's okay to sometimes agree to disagree. It doesn't mean you love each other any less.

DIY: Picture This

A simple token of your affection can win you major brownie points with the parentals! I love this little art project that recycles jar lids into fridge magnets. Put a fave photo of your family inside and hand them out at the holidays or on Mother's Day or Father's Day.

✳ ❀ ✳ ❀ ✳ ❀ ✳ ❀ ✳ ❀ ✳ ❀ ✳

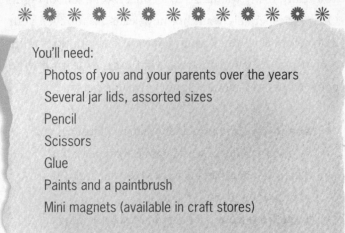

You'll need:
   Photos of you and your parents over the years
   Several jar lids, assorted sizes
   Pencil
   Scissors
   Glue
   Paints and a paintbrush
   Mini magnets (available in craft stores)

1. Place the lids on the back of the photos. Trace the shape of the lids on the back of the center of the photos.
2. Cut the photos out and glue inside the lids.
3. With paints, decorate each lid. Let dry for thirty minutes.
4. Glue a magnet to the back of each lid. Now put them on your fridge where your parents will be sure to see them!

✳ ❀ ✳ ❀ ✳ ❀ ✳ ❀ ✳ ❀ ✳ ❀ ✳

Can We Talk? Communicating with Your Mom and Dad

You really, really wanna go to a concert on a school night. Or you desperately want hot new jeans . . . or even your own room! The way I see it, you've got two options. Hire a high-priced lawyer to argue your case, or learn how to come across as a mature, knowledgeable person.

- ◆ **Ask away.** Seriously, a lot of kids will just agonize over something for weeks rather than put it out there. Tell your parents what you want and why it's so important to you.

- ◆ **Build your case.** Telling your parents you need the latest phone "because it's so cool!" isn't going to get you very far. Do some research, so you can explain clearly what's involved (price, time commitment, maintenance, etc.). I know one girl who really wanted a dog and did a schedule to show her parents how she would take care of it (walking, feeding, grooming, etc.). They were so impressed . . . they caved!

- ◆ **Hear them out.** Don't just stomp out of the room if they initially say no. Listen to their side of the argument. What are their concerns/hesitations?

Is there anything you can do to make them more comfortable? Is there any compromise you can all agree upon? Throwing a tantrum is not a good way to get what you want; acting like a mature adult is.

♦ **Let them think it over.** Don't demand an answer right away. Present your argument, then tell your parents to take some time to consider it before giving you their answer. This will show them how serious (and not impulsive!) you are.

♦ **Accept their decision gracefully.** No whining. No arguing. If you want something in the future, honor your parents' wishes now—even if you don't agree with them. A little respect will go a long, long way.

Heart to Heart: Asking Your Parents for Advice

Once upon a time, your mom and dad were actually tweens. Believe it or not, they dealt with a lot of the same stuff you're going through (even if it was way back in the Dark Ages!). I know opening up to your parents about your fears or feelings can be pretty awkward. Some stuff (like crushes and body changes) just feels so personal and embarrassing! But give them a try—they can be a great source of support and good advice. Besides, who knows you longer and better than they do?

- **Pick a parent.** If you're not comfortable talking to both parents at once, then choose one depending on the subject you need to discuss. My dad is great with business stuff—he'll give me his honest opinion on a song or a script. My mom is awesome with daily "drama"—the stuff that I might be worrying about. She can put it all into perspective for me.

- **Timing is everything!** If your dad is watching the World Series or your mom is busy balancing her checkbook, then that is not the best time to broach a difficult subject. Wait until you have their one-hundred-percent undivided attention—no distractions!

- **Be honest if you're uncomfortable.** You can say, "Mom, this isn't easy for me to talk to you about . . . " so she knows this is important to you.

- **Ask how they handled it.** Chances are, your mom or dad has gone through a similar experience. Maybe they can recall what it was like; how they felt and acted. Was there something they wish they had known or done?

◆ **Make a regular "talk time."** Schedule in a few minutes every day (before bedtime or over breakfast in the a.m. works for me) to chat with your parents. Stuff comes up every day, and it's nice to know I can run things by my parents as I am dealing with them.

*Just Askin':
Growing pains

My dad doesn't think I'm old enough to walk home from school by myself. But I'm twelve years old!

This is a good time to show, not tell. Show your dad you are mature and responsible enough to take on this task. Ask him if maybe you can do a few "test walks." Have him walk behind you a few feet and observe you as you cross streets, carefully looking both ways and waiting for the "walk" signal on traffic lights. Show him how safe you can be in everything else you do: always buckle your seat belt, never talk to strangers, and obey all family rules. You can also suggest walking home with a friend who lives nearby. Eventually, when he sees you can be trusted, he'll give you your walking papers!

My mom keeps buying me clothes that are really embarrassing, not cool. Last week, it was a pink kitty shirt! Does she still think I'm a baby?

I think secretly your parents are always going to see you as a baby because you *are* their baby. I know it's hard because you don't want to hurt your mom's feelings by telling her to back off, but you have to do something to solve this fashion emergency! Gently sit her down and say you are older now and your style has changed. Maybe you guys can even go shopping together so she can get a better idea of your fashion sense. As for the kitty shirt . . . save it for Halloween!

To Sum It Up:

While you're struggling to be more independent, your mom and dad are having a tough time letting go. It's a hard time for everyone in the family, so don't be surprised if conflicts come up. It's not the end of the world! Just remember to treat your folks the way you want them to treat you (can you say "R-E-S-P-E-C-T"?). They love you and will always give you a shoulder to lean on (or cry on!) when things get complicated and crazy.

P.S.

Chapter 10

If You Can Dream It, You Can Do It

Even as a little girl, I had big dreams. I knew I wanted to be an entertainer.

I could see myself singing and dancing in front of millions of people. There has never been a moment I have wanted to give up, even when I hit a few bumps in the road along the way. I just knew that any dream was within my reach if I believed in myself. Achievers are also great dreamers.

So what do you dream of? Ask yourself this: if you could be anything, what would you choose? Maybe you want to be a pro basketball player or a rock star . . . a best-selling author . . . a scientist . . . a ballerina . . . an astronaut. I say, go for it! Now is the time in your life to explore all your options and fantasize about what your future might hold. The coolest thing about being a tween is that your life is just beginning to get exciting! You have so many choices, so many opportunities—and none of the responsibility of being a grown-up yet. Enjoy it!

Your dreams may change as you get older, and that's okay, too. Mine are definitely evolving! I want to design my own line of clothing—and maybe even accessories, jewelry, and shoes, too! That might not have been in my original game plan, but I'm adding it to my "to-do" list. That's another great thing about dreams—there's always room for more.

Zendaya's Dream List

- ☑ Go to college
- ☒ Headline a sold-out world concert tour!
- ☒ Work with Beyoncé
- ☒ Be interviewed by Oprah
- ☑ Travel the world
- ☐ Start my own charity to help kids and schools
- ☐ Win an Oscar and a Grammy
- ☒ Break a world record
- ☒ Be a best-selling author! :-)

Make It Happen

A dream is a vision and, to quote Cinderella, it's a wish your heart makes. But to make it come true takes action, dedication, and sacrifice. I missed a lot of fun things at school while I was pursuing my dreams, and it was difficult not being able to see my mom and my dog all the time while I lived in L.A. It was hard on me, but when I meet my fans in the audience at *Shake It Up* or rock out at one of my concerts, I know it was totally worth it! I get to do what I love all the time.

A lot of kids ask me how I got into show business. My answer is always the same: persistence. I just kept at it until the right role found me and I found it. Did it happen overnight? No way. That stuff rarely happens. You gotta work hard to make your dreams a reality. If you want to win a gold medal in swimming in the Olympics, you have to practice your laps every day. If you want to act on Broadway, you gotta take drama classes. Hard work is behind every win. But I think that's a good thing. If everything I have today was just handed to me, I wouldn't appreciate it as much as I do. I'm proud of how far I've come because I know how hard I worked to get here.

Get a goal. Start with a small goal at first, something that's attainable. Say you want to be a fashion designer:

begin by learning how to sew or sketch. Then, when you're ready, set a long-term goal—something that might take a little more time and work. Setting my small goal was simple: I needed to go on auditions and get an agent. A producer wasn't going to knock on my door and hand me a starring role! I had to go out and read for casting and convince people to hire me. My long-term goal was to break into show biz and be the best that I could be. I knew I wanted to be up there with Beyoncé!

Keep your eyes on the prize. By this I mean don't give up too easily if things don't happen as quickly as you'd like. I think we all get let down. There have been tons of roles in my life that I haven't gotten. I had to go through three Disney auditions before I landed on *Shake It Up*. Before that, I probably went through dozens. Who knows—I lost count! But I always believed that my dream would eventually happen for me. Persistence pays off. Be determined and remember that life is filled with opportunity. Tomorrow is another day. I love this saying: "It's not a matter of if; it's a matter of when."

Tune out the critics. You know who I mean. The haters who tell you it can't be done or you're wasting your time. If it's your dream and your passion, let nothing and no one stand in your way. It's beautiful if you can look past all the "nos" and just get to that "yes."

Be flexible. Opportunity knocks when you least expect it! I was planning to audition for CeCe and had already learned her lines—when the producers asked me to try for Rocky. So I was like, "Okay, sure, I'll read for that." I was open to it. I was willing to give it a shot. I went out to the car, studied my lines for twenty minutes, and came back and read for Rocky. I'm so glad I did, because it obviously turned out great for me. Sometimes you can reach your destination by taking a totally different road. Is there another way you can make your dream come true? If you want to be an actress, why not explore other aspects of filmmaking, like lighting or costume design?

DIY: A Dream Collage

Create a collage of images and words and surround yourself with positive inspiration! Your collage should remind you of what you want to be, and how it will feel to get there. Pin yours up where can you easily see it—like over your bed or by your desk.

✳ ❀ ✳ ❀ ✳ ❀ ✳ ❀ ✳ ❀ ✳ ❀ ✳

You'll need:
  Poster board
  Scissors
  A stack of different magazines (women's, teen,
    health, news, nature, etc.)
  Glue stick

Look through your magazines and cut out images, words, and phrases that remind you of your dream. For example, if you want to be a veterinarian, then you might find the word "heal" or "care" and photos of cute kittens and puppies. If your goal is to be a champion tennis player, then you might clip out pics of Venus and Serena and the phrase "Tennis is my racquet." You can add more to your collage every day; make it a work in progress!

✳ ❀ ✳ ❀ ✳ ❀ ✳ ❀ ✳ ❀ ✳ ❀ ✳

✳ Just Askin':
Future imperfect

I have no idea what I want to be when I grow up!

You have a lot of time to figure out what you want to be when you grow up. So don't worry about it now. Instead, try lots of things. Don't be afraid! The worst thing you'll find out is that you don't like it, or maybe there's something you're even better at. I'll let you in on a little secret: hardly anyone starts off being good at things right off the bat. Look for something that's fun and makes you happy. That will be your clue to your future profession! Passion is what makes people successful. If you do what you love, you can't fail.

I want to quit gymnastics! It's been seven years, and I'm so tired of taking it, but I'm afraid my mom won't let me.

You have to be honest with your mom. Explain calmly that it's just not your passion anymore and you'd like to try something else for a change. Assure her that you're not just throwing in the towel; you've given this a lot of thought and you feel you need to move on. Maybe you want to stop gymnastics so you can try karate. Let her know you have a plan, so she understands you're not just quitting, you're expanding your horizons.

Inspiration . . .

A POEM BY ZENDAYA

Inspiration
That glimmer of brilliance
That crashing wave in your
 subconscious
A firecracker pop in your cranium
 when ideas are your aliens
That shock to your fingertips, urging
 you to genius
Inspiration
An undefined feeling
When words have a meaning
When songs are worth singing
When air is worth breathing
Inspiration
Your tummy, which holds all those
 butterflies
The twinkle in one's eyes
A baby's whines and cries
A lover's good-byes
It can be seen from the skies
Heard from the mountain highs
Touched through numbed pain
And smelled through pouring rain
Are you
Inspired?

Inspiration Is Everywhere!

Whenever I find myself stuck in a rut—or feeling a little lazy and unmotivated—I scope around for some inspiration. It hits you when you least expect it, and there's no knowing what direction it will come from. You can't force yourself to find it; you can't Google it or find it on a map. You just have to be open and let inspiration come to you.

Kind of like my poem. I had no clue what I was going to write when I put pencil to paper. So I closed my eyes and let the words come to me. Not only did I write the poem, I discovered how I was going to end my book with this chapter by helping to inspire you to achieve your dreams!

So maybe you don't know just yet what your dream is—that's okay! While you're trying to discover your passion, allow yourself to be inspired. Here are some helpful tips to get there:

◆ **Invent your motto.** Mine came to me pretty easily: "DFTS: Don't Forget to Smile." This simple phrase really inspires me to keep pushing forward and reaching for my dreams, and it captures my positive outlook. You might prefer "Reach for the stars," "Breathe," or even "Never wrestle with a pig"—whatever works for you! If the words speak to you and connect you with your inner strength and determination, it should be your motto. Post it on your Facebook page, wear it on a T-shirt, or shout it to the world!

◆ **Don't waste a moment.** I admit it: I like to be a little lazy sometimes. Don't you? I enjoy sleeping in, hangin' out in my PJs all day, and eating ice cream straight out of the carton. It's okay to let yourself veg out now and then. But if it's becoming a habit (and you can't remember the last time you showered), you're in trouble. On those days when I'm in a daze, I remind myself that time is so precious and I shouldn't be wasting it. What could you achieve in a minute, an hour, a week, if you didn't dawdle that time away? What if you picked yourself up (instead of procrastinating) and put your mind to a task? It's when I take action that I feel the most empowered and inspired. I tell myself that I want to live my life to the fullest. My goal is to be a performer—not a couch potato!

◆ **Celebrate yourself.** I don't mean throw an "I Love Me" party (although if you've got the space, go for it!). I mean applaud your victories, no matter how small. Pat yourself on the back and remind yourself of your "Happy Time," when you were able to shine. Maybe it was winning your school spelling bee . . . or landing a spot on the soccer team . . . or singing a solo in your choir. Connect with that feeling of pride and joy and let it inspire you even more. My Happy Time was a concert in Arizona when I performed in front of eight thousand people. Talk about amazing! I just think about it, and I feel on top of the world. I celebrated that moment pretty much the same way I celebrate most good times with my family: we just hang and stay up all night talking! For us, we don't need a big ol' party, we just need each other.

♦ **Let your mind wander.** Sometimes, I like to just shut the door to my dressing room, close my eyes, and have myself a think! Some people call it meditation. For me, it's just letting myself be still and quiet so inspiration can come to me. I usually crank up a tune, and that mellows me out. Let ideas come to you, then jot them down after. You'd be surprised what your brain will dream up if you give it some space!

✳ Just Askin':
Keepin' the faith

I feel like I'm a disaster! No matter what I do, I stink at it! I'm not good at sports, I'm not artistic, and I can't carry a tune!

Dude, lose the negative 'tude. If you go into everything you try expecting to fail, then guess what? You will! It's very important to have faith in yourself. Instead of saying "I can't do it," tell yourself, "There's nothing I can't do." Sometimes you can be your own worst enemy, sabotaging your opportunities before you've given yourself a chance to succeed. Any time my inner Debbie Downer starts to kick in, I give myself a little pep talk. It's kind of a weird thing to do, but you just sit there and say, "I'm awesome!" and let yourself really, truly believe it. I promise you, you will find your talent. Everyone has something that makes them special and unique.

I auditioned for a play . . . and totally blew it! How will I ever become an actress if I panic and mess up?

There have been lots of times when I've flubbed my lines so bad in front of producers and casting agents! One particularly horrible dance audition comes to mind: I danced around and tripped, sending everything on the set falling down around me. I felt like crying and running off stage, but I didn't. I got back up, snapped my fingers, and kept on moving. You know what? I booked that commercial. And it was a great lesson that you can learn from, too. No one is perfect; no one gets it right all the time. But if you can pick yourself up, dust yourself off, and get back on your feet . . . that's perseverance. I make it my rule to learn from every mistake I make. Work on memorizing your lines and calming your nerves so that the next audition will go smoother. And if you "oops" again . . . give yourself a break and laugh it off!

To Sum It Up:

Being a tween can be an awkward time in your life, but you'll get through it! The greatest thing is, you're starting this amazing journey toward adulthood. Let yourself be inspired by everything around you, reach for the stars, and don't ever stop believing in yourself. Remember that the people who love you will always be there to cheer you on (and catch you if you fall!). And I'm a member of your fan club, too! I know you can do anything you set your mind to. Have fun . . . and keep me posted!

Dream Journal

Use this journal to write down your goals
and then how you will make them happen.
Remember, if you can dream it, you can do it!

Acknowledgments

Oh my, there's just too many people to thank here. First and foremost, my beautiful parents for well . . . giving me life . . . I guess, but also for helping me navigate through these past crazy tween (and now teen) years and giving me such solid guidance and advice that I can now proudly share my thoughts and hopefully help someone else. Next my lovely teachers for not only helping through the writing process, but for letting this massive project count toward my English grade! Love to my management team for believing in me the second I walked in the door a few years back! Much love to my Disney family for making all my dreams realities, such as this book! ;) And of course the fabulous Sheryl Berk for listening to all my crazy stories, helping me actually make sense of it all, and turn it into something fun, fresh, and helpful. Thanks a bunch! And last but definitely not least, I want to thank and give a big spirit hug to every single one of my beautiful little ZSWAGGERS for allowing me to live my dream and for supporting me through everything I do. I would be nothing without you. Much love, and DFTS :)

ZENDAYA stars as Rocky Blue on the hit Disney Channel series *Shake It Up*. Zendaya, which means "to give thanks" in Shona (a Bantu language native to the Shona people of Zimbabwe), was a fashion model for Macy's, Mervyn's, and Old Navy. She was also one of the backup dancers in a Sears commercial featuring Disney Channel star Selena Gomez! Zendaya also spent three years dancing with Future Shock Oakland, a hip-hop dance troupe, and two years dancing hula with AHA, the Academy of Hawaiian Arts. Zendaya now resides in Los Angeles, California, with her family and dog, a giant schnauzer named Midnight. Her interests include singing, dancing, and designing clothes.

SHERYL BERK is a *New York Times* best-selling author several times over. She has collaborated with dozens of celebrities on their memoirs, including Britney Spears, Whitney Port, Tia Mowry, and Jenna Ushkowitz. *Soul Surfer,* co-written with Bethany Hamilton, was a #1 best seller and recently a major motion picture. She is the founding and former editor-in-chief of *Life & Style Weekly*. Her ten-year-old daughter, Carrie, got her hooked on *Shake It Up*!